WEIGHT LOSS

The Essential Guide

Sara
Kirkham

First published in Great Britain in 2010 by
Need2Know
Remus House
Coltsfoot Drive
Peterborough
PE2 9BF
Telephone 01733 898103
Fax 01733 313524
www.need2knowbooks.co.uk

Contents

Introduction 5

Chapter 1 Globesity – The New Epidemic 7

Chapter 2 How Do You Measure Up? 15

Chapter 3 Planning for Success 27

Chapter 4 How to Create a Calorie Deficit with Diet ... 35

Chapter 5 Calories – To Count or Not To Count? 51

Chapter 6 Portion Size – Just as Much to Blame! 61

Chapter 7 Weight Loss through Exercise 73

Chapter 8 Weight Loss Tools and Gimmicks 89

Chapter 9 Weight Loss for Life 101

Chapter 10 Recipes 117

Help List 125

Book List 130

References 131

Appendix 133

Introduction

In a world saturated with dietary advice, this book is a source of credible information and indispensable, practical weight loss tips, providing all the tools you will need to achieve successful long-term weight loss.

It has been estimated that almost 50% of women are dieting most of the time, with 13 million people on a permanent diet. Yet despite these figures, we aren't getting any slimmer – obesity is a disease epidemic. Many people following a weight loss regime will falter within the first few weeks, regain any weight lost and resume with an alternative diet plan, only to fail again. This book is for every person still looking for the ultimate guide that will enable them to lose weight and maintain it.

Although the science behind weight loss is simple (i.e. if you take in fewer calories than you use up, you will lose weight), weight loss is certainly not easy to achieve for most people. There are countless issues and pressures that contribute to our food choices, and making dietary and lifestyle changes is inherently difficult. We tend to set goals that are too ambitious, follow diets that cannot be maintained and quickly become disillusioned with the results. This book will enable you to understand weight gain and weight loss – it discusses the lifestyle pitfalls that contribute to weight gain, will help you to identify your own personal dietary or lifestyle gremlins that cause healthy eating plans to fail, and enable you to take stock of where you are and set achievable diet and exercise goals to achieve success.

You have found the perfect tool in *Weight Loss – The Essential Guide* if you want to:

- Find out your starting point body mass index (BMI), waist circumference or waist-hip ratio.
- Learn how to set realistic weight loss goals that are more likely to be successful.
- Maximise your chances of weight loss success.
- Reduce calorie intake without being 'on a diet'.

- Learn how to shop for, prepare and enjoy healthy foods.

- Try new recipes.

- Understand how to control your appetite, blood sugar levels and eating behaviours, and get back in control of what you eat.

- Understand the psychology behind changing your eating behaviour.

- Discover how to begin and stick with a long-term exercise regime to promote weight loss.

Disclaimer

This book is not intended to replace professional medical advice, although it can be used alongside the advice of your GP. If you are considering making dietary or lifestyle changes, you are recommended to consult a qualified professional such as a nutritionist or dietitian, and if you have any health issues or are obese, it is recommended that you consult a healthcare professional before embarking on any dietary or exercise regime changes.

Chapter One

Globesity – The New Epidemic

Weight loss is big business. The National Obesity Forum reports that 20% of people in the UK are classed as obese, an estimated 300 million people around the world are obese (International Obesity Task Force, 2010), and the World Health Organisation predicts that by 2015 approximately 2.3 billion adults worldwide will be overweight, and more than 700 million of those will be obese. It is an epidemic caused by an increased intake of energy-dense foods that are high in fat and sugars, together with a reduction in physical activity. Many foods have increased in calories (energy density), while changes in transport, work and leisure activities have resulted in lower energy expenditure. Our energy balance equation no longer balances up.

A growing problem

The energy balance equation is simple: if calories 'in' are greater than calories 'out', we gain weight. However, weight loss may be simple in theory, but it is not necessarily easy in practice. Changing our eating and lifestyle habits is often difficult to do, and is not always helped by all the weight loss and dieting information available. Magazines, diet books, celebrity diets, television programmes and the Internet all provide a vast and constantly changing source of information about how to lose weight – but which sources can you trust?

With increasing numbers of clinically and morbidly obese individuals, the task of helping people to reduce body weight has expanded from the realms of weight loss groups and health centres and is now also a medical issue, with very low-calorie diets monitored by GPs becoming the norm.

The promise of quick results entices us to follow harsh and unhealthy diets that may initially create weight loss (though not necessarily loss of body fat), but are not sustainable for any length of time. So we return to our normal eating pattern and gain any lost weight back, then look for the next diet to try.

Why do we get fat?

Body fat, also known as adipose tissue, accumulates when we take in more calories than we use up. It's a simple equation known as the energy balance equation: for weight maintenance, calories in must equal calories out. However, calculating how many calories you take in and how many are used up in energy is difficult, and managing it, for many people, seems almost impossible.

Having such a wide range of taste-enhanced, cheap food available is too much of a temptation for many of us, and when coupled with food marketing gimmicks such as 'two for one' and tasty snacks placed at crucial locations in supermarkets to tempt us into buying them, eating healthily can sometimes feel like an uphill struggle.

On top of this, our lives revolve around food – as a society we have recognised meal times whether we are hungry or not, business lunches and sandwich runs in the office, and events throughout the year where indulgence is not only accepted but expected e.g. Christmas and Easter.

If you have ever dieted before, you will know that there is always something around the corner that gets in the way of your diet or healthy eating plan. Many people do not eat to live, but live to eat! Food is no longer just an energy source: we use food for comfort and for social acceptance, we eat and drink to celebrate and commiserate, and we even eat to congratulate or punish our dieting achievements and downfalls.

How do we get fat?

When excess food is consumed, anything that cannot be used by the body will be converted into body fat and stored. We can convert excess carbohydrates, proteins or fats into body fat, but it takes much more energy to convert carbohydrates and proteins into body fat. For example, if the body takes in 100 excess calories of fat, it can be converted and stored as body fat using only 2-3 calories of energy, whereas if the body takes in 100 excess calories of carbohydrate, it can be converted and stored as body fat using up 23 calories.

Body fat is stored in cells called adipocytes. Although increased food intake and higher body fat levels during childhood can multiply the number of fat cells we develop, once into adulthood the number of fat cells we have generally remains the same. However, each fat cell will grow in size as it stores more fat inside (see diagram).

Adipose cell (adipocyte)
containing a fat droplet

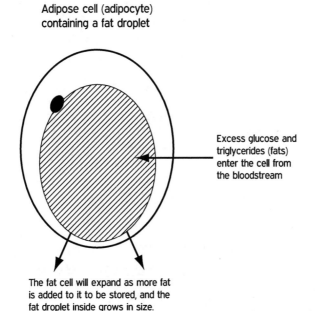

Excess glucose and triglycerides (fats) enter the cell from the bloodstream

The fat cell will expand as more fat is added to it to be stored, and the fat droplet inside grows in size.

'When excess food is consumed, anything that cannot be used by the body will be converted into body fat and stored.'

We can store a lot of energy as body fat because it is stored without water, so it is relatively lightweight and compact. There are approximately 3,500 calories in 1lb of body fat, so to remove this amount of fat we have to create an energy deficit of slightly less than 3,500 calories, either by eating less or exercising more. The deficit is slightly less as we use some of this energy up just converting the stored fat back into triglycerides to break it down for energy.

More fat cells or just bigger fat cells?

With increasing amounts of research in this field, two patterns of obesity are emerging. It seems that the body fat of obese individuals may be:

- Hyperplastic – an increased number of fat cells which may be a normal size or an increased size.

- Hypertrophic – a normal number of fat cells but with larger amounts of fat stored inside.

The number of fat cells formed is determined at an early age. However, the size of the fat cells is determined at a later age, so although a greater number of fat cells may increase the likelihood of gaining weight, this will only happen if you take in more energy than is required and store the excess in these fat cells.

Nature vs nurture

If you live in an environment where obesity is common, there is an increased chance that you will also gain excess weight. The eating habits picked up during our childhood contribute to our lifetime eating habits.

Think back to your childhood

- Were food portions large?

- Were you encouraged to finish your plate, regardless of how full you felt?

- Did you have to finish your main meal before you could have a dessert?

- Were all meals finished with something sweet?

- Was confectionery used as treats?

- Were meals rushed or eaten on the go, encouraging you to eat quickly?

All of these behaviours contribute to poor eating habits, encouraging overeating, eating too quickly to recognise and respond to feeling full, or creating a sweet tooth in later years. We tend to continue with known and preferred eating habits until there is either a deliberate or life-changing occurrence in our life. This can be a decision to change eating habits for weight loss or health reasons, but is just as likely to be a change in job, moving home to live with a new partner or different family member, going to university or living abroad, for example.

As the number of fat cells we have remains largely unchanged, if we take in excess calories these fat cells become larger, and if we reduce our energy intake the cells will still remain but will shrink.

What do I have to gain by losing weight?

Several health conditions are caused or exaggerated by excess body fat levels, including Type 2 diabetes, insulin resistance and metabolic syndrome, coronary heart disease, osteoarthritis, liver diseases and some types of cancer. Body fat, particularly if stored around the middle, also releases inflammatory substances into the body which can cause further health complications.

In addition to the physical stresses on the body, our body shape affects the way we feel about ourselves and causes a range of behavioural problems – from low self-esteem and poor self-confidence to depression. It can affect the way we dress, the way we present ourselves to others and often influences the decisions we make in life, such as whether we feel comfortable going to a fitness class or swimming, or whether we apply for a promotion at work. It also has an effect upon our relationships with other people.

Lose weight – live longer

Being a healthy weight also appears to be linked with living longer. Animal research has shown that calorie restriction can extend life expectancy by one third to twice as long as normal and this is also illustrated in a number of human populations. In some areas of Japan where up to 40% fewer calories are consumed than in other areas, there are more centenarians and much less disease.

'As the number of fat cells we have remains largely unchanged, if we take in excess calories these fat cells become larger, and if we reduce our energy intake the cells will still remain but will shrink.'

Benefits of losing weight

- Reduced risk of disease.
- Increased longevity.
- Improved quality of life.
- Higher self-esteem and improved self-confidence.
- Better body image.
- Better mobility.

Weigh it up

But even once you have acknowledged all the benefits of weight loss, there is still one big hurdle – you will have to make substantial changes to your eating habits and lifestyle in order to be successful – and this is where the sticking point is for most people. Making changes like this is tough and requires will power and support as well as know-how and motivation. That is where this book can help, because here you will find not only a trustworthy source of information, but also an insight into how you can change your eating behaviours for life – and stick with it.

Summing Up

- We gain weight when we take in more calories than we use up.

- Any type of excess food can be converted into body fat and stored.

- We form more fat cells during early and adolescent growth phases.

- Obesity is either a greater number of fat cells or a normal number of fat cells that are filled with more fat.

- Once you have developed additional fat cells, you are stuck with them, but it is the amount of fat you store within these cells that determines your body fat level.

- Being overweight contributes to a number of other disease conditions.

Chapter Two

How Do You Measure Up?

Do I need to lose weight?

There are several ways to measure your weight or the amount of body fat you are carrying. Each measuring option has its own benefits and drawbacks, so just choose a way to measure your weight loss that suits you. As long as the results are going in the right direction, it doesn't matter if you measure overall body weight on weighing scales, girth measurements with a tape measure or body fat percentage.

Although some people carry more muscle and are heavier but not necessarily fatter than others, a reasonable place to assess whether you need to lose weight is a weight-height chart such as the one overleaf.

Another good measure to help you decide whether you are overweight is a waist circumference measurement, which will be explained later in this chapter. However, if you are heavier than you used to be, or your clothes are no longer fitting comfortably, it is likely that you will benefit from returning to a healthier, lower weight.

Your weight in kilos

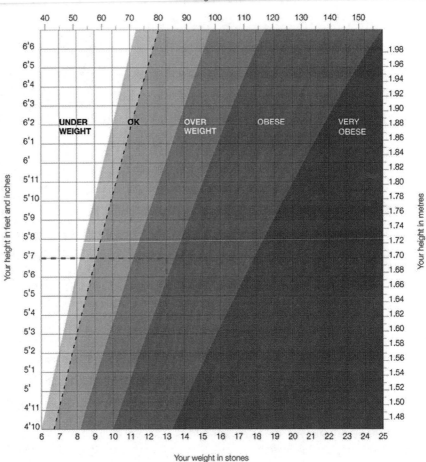

© Crown copyright. Source: Food Standards Agency.

How to measure your weight loss

- Tape measurements – choose from waist circumference, waist-hip ratio or a selection of girth measurements taken from the areas you want to reduce (waist, stomach, hips, thighs, arms, etc).

- Weighing scales.

- Devices measuring body fat percentage.

- Body mass index (BMI).

Benefits and drawbacks of measuring instruments

Type of measurement	Pros	Cons
Tape measurements	Quick and easy.	Can be inaccurate.
Weighing scales	Quick and easy Accurate measure of overall weight loss (dependant upon scales used).	Measures total body weight so it is unknown what type of weight (water weight, body fat or muscle) has been lost.
BMI	Easy with web-based BMI calculators.	Only based upon weight and height – can provide an 'overweight' reading for heavy-muscled individuals.
Body fat measurements	Measures changes in body fat, which is the type of tissue you ideally want to lose.	Measures are affected by hydration levels, which can be difficult to keep the same to monitor accurate changes.

Tape measurements

This sounds really simple and it is one of the quickest and easiest ways to monitor your progress as you lose weight. However, it can be inaccurate if not done carefully, lifting spirits one month only to drop you into despair when you appear to have gained back the inches you thought you had already lost.

Considerations for an accurate tape measurement

- Take measurements on bare skin – clothes make measurements inaccurate and can easily add centimetres to a measurement, and you won't remember what you wore in your last measure up.

- Note the exact spot that you are measuring – use clear 'body landmarks' to line up your tape measure, such as the belly button for a waist measurement or the hip bones for a hip measurement. For arm and leg measurements, you can measure how many inches/centimetres from the crotch or elbow your measuring point is, or use birthmarks/tattoos to help line your tape measure up. Write down exactly where you measured so you can repeat the measurement in the same place.

- Take up any slack in the tape measure and make sure it isn't twisted.

- Have someone else take the measurements – as well as this being much more accurate, they are more likely to be objective (and not pull the tape measure in tighter on subsequent measurements!).

- Take the measurement without looking at the previous figure – seeing what you were last week/last month may lead you to inadvertently moving the tape measure around until you find a measurement that is slightly less.

- Don't attempt to hold in your stomach – you're only cheating yourself!

- Take the measurements at the same time of day if possible, avoiding obvious things that could affect a net change in girth measurements such as measuring immediately after eating.

- Keep a clear record of your measurements in a diary, on a calendar or on a sheet of paper kept in a safe place – figures jotted down on a scrap of paper are too easily lost and you will not remember measurements from a month ago.

Remember, as you lose body fat from all over your body, you will lose different amounts from different areas. Doing girth measurements will give you an idea of where you are losing the most weight from. Contrary to popular belief, you cannot choose to reduce body fat from specific areas of the body, although you can tone up the muscle in targeted parts of the body.

Waist circumference

Body fat held around the thighs and bottom is not as much of a health risk as excess body fat stored around the middle. Central obesity increases the fat levels in the liver's blood supply, decreasing the liver's sensitivity to insulin and contributing to the development of Type 2 diabetes. Body fat stored around the middle also increases the production of 'bad' cholesterol in the liver, which contributes to coronary heart disease. So, it is a good idea to keep your waist circumference within specific circumference guidelines, and this provides an easy-to-measure goal for weight loss and improved health.

Knowing your waist circumference or waist-hip ratio can help you to discover whether you are storing excess calories around the middle, and also gives you an easy way to measure your weight loss. Here are the recommended guidelines suggested by the NHS.

Waist circumference guidelines for women	Waist circumference guidelines for men
Ideal: less than 80cm (32in). High: 80cm to 88cm (32 to 35in). Very high: more than 88cm (35in).	Ideal: less than 94cm (37in). High: 94cm to 102cm (37 to 40in). Very high: more than 102cm (40in).

How to measure your waist circumference

Locate the top of your hip bone on one side of the body and then locate the bottom of your ribs on the same side. Halfway between the two bones is your waist – this will usually be at around the same level as your bellybutton and at the narrowest part of your torso. You may find it easier to do this (and to see the tape measurement) using a mirror.

'The "apple" shape is less desirable than the "pear" shape as far as health goes – body fat around the abdomen is linked with increased risk of Type 2 diabetes, coronary heart disease and inflammatory endocrine disorders.'

The Ashwell® Shape Chart below illustrates how your waist measurement might be affecting your health. This could be used as an additional motivational tool as you lose weight and move from one section of the chart to another.

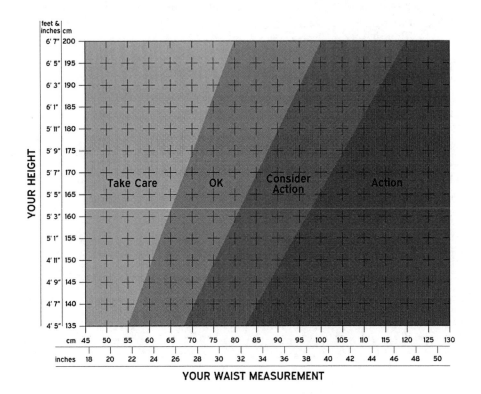

© Dr Margaret Ashwell.

Waist-hip ratio

The waist-hip ratio compares the circumference of your waist to your hips – the greater your waist circumference is in comparison to your hips (the more 'apple' shaped you are), the higher the level of central obesity and health risks.

Need2Know

Waist-hip ratios

Women	Men
Ideal: less than 0.8 Too high: 0.85 or more	Ideal: less than 0.9 Too high: 1 or more

How to calculate your waist-hip ratio

To calculate your waist-hip ratio, simply divide your waist measurement by your hip measurement.

$$\frac{\text{Waist measurement}}{\text{Hip measurement}}$$

Make sure that both measurements are either in inches or in centimetres.

To calculate your waist-hip ratio online, go to www.besthealth.com/besthealth/wellness/waisthip.htm.

Weighing scales

Probably the most widely used and convenient device for measuring weight loss is weighing scales. However, when you step onto a set of scales you are weighing everything – muscle, bone mass, water and body fat – so if you are quite muscular, your weight in comparison to someone else can appear quite heavy, yet you may not be overweight. Muscle is much heavier than fatty tissue, so the more muscle you have, the heavier you will be. Conversely, fatty tissue is stored without added water and doesn't weigh as much for the same volume of muscle, one reason why weight (fat) loss on the scales can seem so slow. As with other forms of measurement, scales can also be inaccurate, so take these tips into account for a fair measure:

▪ For scales with a needle gauge, always make sure the pointer is set to zero before you get on.

'A high waist-hip ratio is directly linked with increased risk of coronary heart disease.'

- If you can't see where the needle is from where you are standing, have someone else take the reading. This will be more accurate anyway, as the angle at which you look at the needle can affect your reading.

- For electronic scales, if the measurement seems to fluctuate or is much more or less than expected, check the battery.

- Always stand upright – leaning forwards or backwards often affects the result.

- Weigh yourself naked if possible to omit any weight changes due to heavy clothes or shoes. If it's not possible to weigh yourself naked, at least remove shoes and heavy items of clothing.

- Stand weighing scales on a solid floor surface such as wood or stone rather than carpet, and always weigh yourself on the same scales and the same floor surface.

- Always weigh yourself at the same time of day for a more accurate idea of net weight loss; for example, you may weigh much lighter first thing in the morning before eating anything. The important thing is to be consistent, whatever time of day you weigh yourself.

What should my weight be?

You can use the weight/height chart shown on page 16, but remember that the more muscle you have, the heavier you will weigh on the scales. Due to this anomaly, you may want to do one of two things:

- Use an additional form of measurement to assess changes in body shape, such as tape measurements.

- Just use weight measurements as a start and end point – the main thing is to reduce your weight, rather than worry about where you are in a 'norm' chart, unless your health is at risk, in which case you should consult your GP before embarking on a weight loss regime.

It is useful to know your weight in stones, pounds and kilograms – use the calculation table overleaf to convert your weight from stones into pounds and kilos. The example weight of 10st 8lb has been used to show how the calculation works.

Weight	Formula	Weight
10st 8lb	10st x 14 + 8lb =	148lb
148lb	148lb ÷ 2.2 =	62.27kg

Use the table below to make a note of your weight in the different units of measurements below:

	Your weight
Kg	
St and lb	
Lb	

BMI

One way to find out if you need to lose weight is to calculate your BMI. However, it is important to remember that this measurement is based upon your height and weight alone, and is another measure that does not take into account the amount of muscle that you have. For example, if you exercise regularly, the extra muscle will increase your weight, yet you may carry less body fat than someone of the same weight as you. If your BMI seems unduly high, it may be worth having your body fat levels checked with a health and fitness professional, or using a set of scales that measure body fat as well as weight.

Calculating your BMI

The easiest way to calculate your BMI is to input your weight and height into a web-based BMI calculator and let it work it out for you! Try this one on the Food Standards Agency website at www.eatwell.gov.uk/healthydiet/healthyweight/bmicalculator.

Remember, if you have lots of muscle, you may appear to be overweight when in fact you are not.

If you do not have access to the Internet, you can also calculate your BMI by doing the following:

$$\text{Weight in kg} \div \text{height in m}^2 = \text{BMI}$$

(You need to calculate your height squared by multiplying it by itself, e.g. 1.5m x 1.5m = 2.25.)

BMI of 18-24.9 is desirable.

BMI of 25-30 is considered overweight.

BMI of 30+ is considered obese.

BMI of 40+ is considered morbidly obese.

Body fat measurements

There are several devices that measure body fat levels – most of the home measurement devices use something called 'impedance'. A very light electrical current is sent around the body, usually from one foot to the other, or from fingertips to toes, and the speed of the current is measured. An electrical current travels at different speeds through fatty tissue, muscle, bone and water, and so estimations about the proportion of water, muscle and body fat are made and displayed on the measuring device. The actual weights of water, muscle and body fat given are based upon the proportions of each type of tissue from the impedance results, so your hydration level (the amount of water in the body) can affect the results significantly. It is recommended that you maintain adequate hydration for each measurement. Accurate changes in body fat levels can only be gathered if hydration levels are kept fairly constant.

Some weighing scales have in-built impedance, enabling you to measure total body weight, muscle and body fat levels easier and more quickly. Other body fat devices by BodyStat or Omron need attaching to hands and feet, or can be hand held. These measure impedance through the body without total body weight (which is entered separately).

The benefits of measuring body fat are:

* As you only want to lose body fat and not muscle, this allows you to monitor the type of weight you are losing.

* When overall weight loss is slow this can be very frustrating – knowing that muscle weight has increased but body fat levels have dropped is very motivating, as this will increase metabolism and assist further weight loss

Many 'fad' diets result in weight loss through reductions in water or muscle weight, or reduced stores of carbohydrate. This may look good on the scales, but it does not show a reduction in body fat and the weight is often regained very easily as soon as fluids or carbohydrates are taken in. Measuring and monitoring body fat levels can help you to lose weight more gradually and prevent drastic reductions in water, carbohydrate and muscle, which are all counterproductive to a long-term reduction in body fat and maintained weight loss.

Summing Up

- Choose a type of measurement that you have easy access to, make sure measurements are accurate and that you record what they are and when they were taken.

- Choosing more than one type of measurement can reveal a more accurate picture of changes in body shape. It can also provide ongoing motivation when one measurement appears to show no or little change, but another measurement shows clear progress.

Chapter Three

Planning for Success

The biggest question on everyone's lips is how to lose weight and keep it off – the solution is simple, but not necessarily easy! However, with a little know-how you can create your own weight loss plan and go on to balance calorie intake and expenditure for successful, lifelong weight maintenance.

Reasons for weight gain

There are three key reasons why we gain weight:

- We eat too many high-calorie foods or foods with hidden calories.

- Our portion sizes are too large – we may be eating the right foods but are simply eating too much of them.

- We aren't active enough to use up the calories we have consumed. This is common when a change in job or lifestyle has resulted in lower activity levels, and we haven't adjusted our diet to reduce calorie intake accordingly.

Before we look at how you're going to reduce your calorie intake, or increase your energy expenditure, you need to set your first weight loss goal. Once you know how much weight you plan to lose, you'll also know what sort of calorie deficit you have to achieve, and this will indicate how many changes need to be made to your usual daily food intake.

How much weight should you lose?

A reasonable guideline for your first weight loss goal is 5% of your body weight. However, if you have a BMI which places you as morbidly obese, you may be able to safely lose 10% of your body weight, but in this case you should consult your GP before embarking on a change of diet or exercise regime.

Calculating how much weight to lose

You can calculate 5% of your body weight by doing the following calculation:

$$\text{Weight (lb or kg)} \times 5 \div 100 = 5\% \text{ of body weight}$$

This figure provides your first weight loss goal. If you plan to lose this weight over a six week period, it will be broken down into more manageable chunks.

Six weeks is a good time period to use when setting short-term goals. Remember, this is just your first mini-weight loss goal and does not necessarily represent the total amount of weight you might want to lose.

If 5% of your current weight divided over six weeks comes to more than 2lb weekly weight loss, it's worth planning the weight loss over eight weeks, or simply limiting your weekly weight loss to 2lb to make sure it's realistic. This is because many weight loss goals fail if they are based upon an unachievable weekly weight loss. Don't worry if you would like to lose more weight than this – the goal is not a limit, and any weight lost in addition to the original goal set is a bonus! Here are some helpful guidelines to help you set and achieve your first weight loss goal.

Setting successful weight loss goals

The way to successful weight loss is through making small changes and taking small steps. This way, your lifestyle is less disrupted and you can continue successfully. Once the new changes become habit, you can make further changes. It is a common mistake to aim for the total weight loss you want (e.g. 2st) without breaking it down into smaller goals.

Deciding on your initial weight loss goal

Your initial weight loss goal should be a weight that you can realistically lose over a six week period. A common goal is to lose 1-2lb a week. However, when you consider how much of a calorie loss you would have to achieve in order to lose 2lb a week, you may reconsider. There are approximately 3,500 calories in 1lb of body fat. So to lose 2lb of body fat a week, you have to create a calorie deficit of approximately 7,000 calories over that week, or eat 1,000 calories less a day! This is a tall order for most people, and is unrealistic unless you have a lot of weight to lose or are currently consuming a very high-calorie diet. Even losing 1lb a week requires a calorie deficit of 3,500 calories a week, or 500 calories daily.

It's also worth considering that the less weight you have to lose, the less body fat you are likely to lose each week. So if you have a stone or less to lose, aim for a smaller loss such as ½ lb weekly. It's better to achieve the goal you originally set, rather than begin with an unrealistic target and then fail. A loss of ½ lb weekly would still create an overall weight loss of nearly ½ st over 12 weeks. Later on we'll look at your food diary to see where you might find calories to cut out, but for now, let's agree on your weight loss goal.

'SMART goals can increase your chance of success by up to 20%.'

SMART goals

Setting SMART goals for weight loss will increase your chances of success. SMART stands for goals that are:

- Specific.
- Measurable.

- ▦ Achievable.

- ▦ Realistic.

- ▦ Time-bound.

Setting your SMART weight loss goal

- ▦ Choose a specific goal, such as the weight you want to be at the end of six weeks, a lower waist measurement or a reduced body fat percentage.

- ▦ Make sure it's measurable, and take account of the guidelines for each form of measurement to ensure accurate results. Your measure could be your weight on the scales, a tape measurement or your waist-hip ratio.

- ▦ Make sure your goal is achievable and realistic – although you will naturally want weight loss results as quickly as possible, setting yourself a tough goal is likely to end in failure, which is demotivating and often contributes to comfort eating and further weight gain.

- ▦ Decide on a date by which you will achieve your first weight loss goal – if you have an important event that you would like to lose weight for, such as a wedding, holiday or social occasion, you might want to use this date as your goal if it's within 4-8 weeks.

'Six weeks is thought to be the best period of time for successful goal setting – it's not too far away that you delay your weight loss action, and it is close enough to keep you motivated'.

How do I know if my weight loss goal is realistic?

Gauging whether your weight loss goal is realistic to achieve can be difficult at first. As a general guideline, if your BMI placed you in the very obese category, you may be able to lose 2lb or more weekly – the more weight you have to lose, the easier it is to lose more weight each week. If you are obese, you may be able to lose ½ -1lb weekly, and if you are overweight, just aim for ½ lb a week. You could calculate what 5% of your current body weight is, and use that as an initial weight loss guideline too. As you lose weight, you will become more adept at setting yourself realistic goals as you get to know your body and how much weight you can expect to lose. If you're obese, you should consult with your GP before changing your diet and exercise regime.

Take these things into consideration:

30

- How much you currently weigh and how much weight you have to lose.

- Whether you have already lost weight and at what rate are you currently losing weight each week.

- Whether your weight loss has slowed down or hit a plateau.

- How much exercise you will be able to do.

- How much you are willing to change your diet.

- Whether there is anything that might get in the way of your weight loss goal, such as social occasions or holidays.

It is important to be realistic and not set an unachievable goal – this is a common error, as we let our hopes override common sense. However, even if you are losing weight, you may lose motivation if you realise you are not going to achieve the weight loss goal you have set for yourself, and this can be detrimental to your success.

For example, if you set a weight loss goal to lose 1st over six weeks and lose 12lb, you may feel disappointed because you didn't hit your weight loss target. However, if you set a weight loss goal of 10lb over six weeks and lose 12lb, you will feel motivated as you over-achieved your target. The weight lost is the same in both examples, but the level of motivation and feeling of achievement is different and may affect whether you continue with your weight loss efforts or not. The idea is not to set a goal that is easy to achieve, but to decide upon an achievable, realistic weight loss goal.

'You are not limited by a realistic weight loss goal – if you lose more weight than you originally planned, this will motivate you even more!'

Write it down and tell others

It's important to write your plans down so that you know what your measurements and goals are, and when you will be measuring your success. Write it in your diary, mark it on the calendar, maybe even plan to treat yourself when you reach your first goal weight. Telling others of your goal may also help you to succeed, as once you have verbalised what you intend to achieve, you are more likely to set out to succeed and meet other people's expectations as well as your own.

Process and outcome goals

The usual way to measure weight loss is with a weight, body fat or tape measurement – these are all known as outcome goals as they measure the end result rather than the process of the goal (what you are doing to achieve the outcome goal).

Research into the success of goal setting has shown that outcome-based goals are likely to be less successful than process-orientated goals for the following reasons:

* The outcome (end result) of a weight loss plan is not entirely in your control, it is only as a result of the process.

* You have to wait a period of time to measure the outcome, and many of us need ongoing motivation to keep us going.

'Measure the journey, not the destination.'

You have more control over process-orientated goals; for example, you can determine how many exercise minutes you complete in a week, but you can't determine exactly how much weight you will lose. If you enjoy the daily/weekly success of achieving what you need to do to lose weight (e.g. exercising or specific dietary changes), this is likely to keep you motivated to stick with your new regime, as well as confirm that you are on track for success.

Of course, you can set yourself both an outcome goal, such as a target weight to get to, and a process goal which determines how you are going to achieve the weight loss. Some process goals are suggested here, with more in the next two chapters on how to lose weight through diet and exercise.

* Complete 180 minutes of exercise each week.

* Limit alcohol units to 10 units per week.

* Swap your usual breakfast to fruit salad every day, or reduce your breakfast cereal portion size to 40g.

You can also set more than one process-orientated goal to help you achieve your outcome (but limit yourself to a maximum of five goals to keep it simple). If you have struggled with achieving weight loss in the past, setting process goals and focusing on the journey rather than the destination could be the key to your success.

Summing Up

So, armed with the following information from this chapter, you are ready to begin your weight loss plan. You know:

▩ How much weight you should aim to lose for your first weight loss target.

▩ How to set a successful weight loss goal.

Remember, your weight loss goal should be SMART for success:

▩ Set a specific goal to achieve.

▩ Decide how you will measure your progress (weight, tape measurements, exercise minutes, etc).

▩ Make sure it's achievable and realistic.

▩ Note down the date that you aim to achieve it by – ideally 4-6 weeks' time.

Chapter Four

How to Create a Calorie Deficit with Diet

There are three ways to create a calorie deficit:

- Reducing your calorie intake.
- Using up more calories through activity and exercise.
- Eating less and exercising more.

Reducing your calorie intake

Rather than randomly cutting foods out of your diet (as in many fad diets), for long-term success it's worth taking a more considered approach. If you cut out all the foods you enjoy eating, your weight loss will be short lived.

The first thing to think about is whether you eat a lot of foods that are high in calories. These are foods such as fatty meats, spreads, dips and oils, alcohol, cakes, biscuits and confectionery. You can check the calorie content of foods at www.weightlossresources.co.uk. However, knowing which foods to avoid and actually avoiding or limiting these foods are two different things! One of the best ways to help you cut calories from your diet is by keeping a food diary. Once you have written down everything that you eat and drink, this helps you to spot where excess calories are being consumed and you can plan how to reduce your daily calorie intake.

'Some experts say that the typical "fad" diet lasts between three days and three weeks – the same length of time as our differing will power!'

Using a food diary

A typical food diary is shown on the next page. You can either copy this, make up one of your own or print one off from one of the websites listed in the help list.

Food diaries have to be completed every day – trying to remember what you have eaten over the last few days is guaranteed to be inaccurate; we often forget much of what we have consumed, particularly snacks and drinks outside of normal meal times. If you prefer to enter your food and drink intake online, visit www.weightlossresrouces.co.uk which automatically calculates your calorie intake. However, this information is only as accurate as the information you enter, so make sure that portion sizes and food selections are correct. Unfortunately, the more accurate you are, the more time consuming this can be.

Keeping a manual food diary at home isn't to calculate daily calorie intake, but simply to help you identify foods or habits which may be contributing to weight gain or inability to lose weight.

Now it's time to figure out where the hidden calories in your diet are, and choose which foods you'd like to reduce to give you the weight loss you want.

Finding high-calorie foods in your food diary

Once you have a few days' worth of food diary in front of you, look out for the following high-calorie foods:

- Full-fat dairy products – cheese, butter, cream, lard, milk and yoghurt.
- High-fat meats, in particular lamb, pork, duck and beef.
- Sauces and dressings (which are usually based upon oils or fats).
- High-fat snacks such as cheese and biscuits, dips or crisps.
- Desserts (apart from meringue without cream, fruit salad, low-fat yoghurts or similar low-calorie desserts).
- Higher-calorie vegetable foods such as nuts, seeds and coconut.
- Alcohol and creamy drinks such as full-fat smoothies or lattes.

Meal	Mon	Tues	Wed	Thurs	Fri	Sat	Sun
Breakfast							
Lunch							
Evening							
Supper							
Snacks							
Fluids							

Some foods, such as butter, cream or fatty meat, are known to be high in calories, but others may come as a surprise. Have a look at the chart below to see the approximate calorie count of some foods.

Food	Average calories in a portion
Peanut butter	Spreading peanut butter on a couple of slices of bread or crackers will add an extra 300 calories to a snack attack!
A packet of sandwiches	Many pre-packed sandwiches pack a heavy punch of around 500 calories, providing a substantial amount of the energy most of us need in a day – and that's before you add a packet of crisps and a drink!
Hummus	Dipping your raw vegetables into a dip like hummus can undo your efforts at choosing a lower calorie snack – a healthy serving can provide well over 300 calories.
Cheese	You may already know that cheese is high in fat and calories, but did you realise that a cubic inch of cheese contains 68 calories, and a cupful of grated cheese over 455 calories?
Potato skins starter with a garlic mayo dip	This tasty starter contains well over 300 calories – before you even tuck into your main meal!
Prawn crackers	Munching away on the free bag of prawn crackers your local takeaway has given you can have you consuming an extra 500 calories on top of your takeaway!

Double cream	Okay, we all know this is one to avoid on any diet, but it's really worth swapping for Greek yoghurt or fromage frais when you know a helping packs in a whopping 372 calories.
Alcohol	A couple of glasses of wine each evening could be adding 250 calories daily, or 1,750 calories over the week.

However, not all high-calorie foods have to be avoided completely. You need to consider how much of each food you are eating, and how many other high-calorie foods you are consuming too. One higher calorie food in a healthy diet is not a problem, as it is the overall calorie intake and calorie expenditure that dictates whether we gain or lose weight. On the other hand, if these foods are your weekly (or even daily) staples, they could be having a significant effect on your waistline. Simply cutting out a couple of glasses of wine in the evening could create enough of a calorie deficit to result in a weight loss of ½lb a week, just from this one change.

You may look at your diet and think you can easily reduce your intake by 500 calories a day. Or you may already be following a reduced-calorie diet or eating healthily and think there is really no room to reduce your intake any lower. You certainly shouldn't consider reducing your calorie intake below your basal metabolic rate (see chapter 5), so if you can't spot ways to easily reduce your calorie intake and keep it within a healthy range, then you need to look for ways to use up more energy through exercise instead.

However, sometimes we underestimate our calorie intake, or fail to spot habits that are detrimental to successful weight loss. For example, if you add a teaspoon of sugar to tea or coffee, this will add approximately 20 calories to each drink. Five drinks a day is adding 100 calories to your daily intake, and this adds up to 700 calories over a week. Getting used to tea or coffee without added sugar is do-able for most people, and will put a significant dint in your calorie intake.

Tips to help you change your diet

Reducing your daily calorie intake by 250 calories can result in a weight loss of approximately ½lb each week. You can do this by, for example:

- Cutting out two large glasses of wine each evening.

- Not adding sugar or honey to drinks and cereals.

- Cutting out a packet of crisps each day.

- Cutting out two biscuits with tea/coffee twice daily.

- Reducing large cereal portions – for example, from 100g to 30g.

Reducing your calorie intake by 500 calories a day can give you a weight loss of 1lb weekly. You can do this by, for example:

- Cutting out a bottle of wine each evening.

- Cutting out four slices of bread or toast with butter or margarine.

- Cutting out cracker and dip snacks throughout the day.

- Cutting out the equivalent of 3-4 matchbox size chunks of cheddar or a similar amount of full-fat cream cheese.

- Eating 150g less starchy carbohydrates such as pasta, rice, potatoes or cereals.

- Not having a weekly takeaway.

The easiest way to adapt your diet without feeling like you are on a diet is to make small changes to lots of aspects of your diet so that you don't miss any one thing too much. By reducing alcohol intake a little, swapping full-fat dairy foods like yoghurt and cheese for low-fat products, not eating buttered bread with meals and cutting down on confectionery and takeaway meals, you can significantly reduce your calorie intake and simultaneously eat a healthier diet.

Although each dietary change only makes a small difference to your calorie intake, changes like this have three benefits:

- You won't feel like you are on a diet when making small changes like this, so you will be able to stick with your new healthy eating regime in the long term.

- In conjunction with other similar dietary adjustments, you will easily and steadily lose weight.

- These changes also promote good health.

Once you have highlighted dietary habits to change on your food diary, you have a number of optional changes you can make:

- You could decide to avoid a certain food or drink altogether.

- You might decide to reduce your intake of certain foods or drinks.

- You might replace that food or drink item with a lower calorie alternative.

Take a look at the examples highlighted on the food diary and the planned changes overleaf.

You don't have to change everything at once – in fact, you're more likely to succeed if you don't make changes too quickly but allow yourself time to adjust to new eating habits. For example, in the food diary overleaf, the portion size of cornflakes hasn't been adjusted and chocolate is still on the menu. Make a list of everything you could change, and then decide which things you will change first.

This way of altering your diet will enable you to slowly lose weight. The more changes you make, the more weight you are likely to lose. However, remember you are in this for the long haul, making smaller changes that you can stick to will enable you to build on your success and stick with it, creating a long-term healthy eating plan that suits you.

There are lots of ways to reduce your daily calorie intake. Have a look at the food diary and choose tips that you think might help you. When each new eating habit becomes a habit that you don't have to think about, choose other changes from the list and add these to your dietary regime.

'Just choose two or three things to adapt and make the changes. Once you are used to these new dietary habits, you are ready to make further changes to your diet.'

	Monday	Tuesday	Wednesday
Breakfast	Big bowl of cornflakes and semi-skimmed milk. Coffee with semi-skimmed milk and two sugars.	Tea with no sugar and semi-skimmed milk.	Pot of yoghurt and fruit. Coffee with semi-skimmed milk and two sugars.
Snacks	Biscuits (2) and coffee with semi-skimmed milk and two sugars.	Biscuits (2) and coffee with semi-skimmed milk and two sugars.	Biscuits (2) and coffee with semi-skimmed milk and two sugars.
Lunch	Lentil and veggie soup with bread and butter. Stick of celery and hummus. Coffee with semi-skimmed milk and two sugars.	Wholemeal bread, tuna and salad sandwich. Orange juice.	Coffee with semi-skimmed milk and two sugars.
Dinner	Large portion of lasagne, salad, garlic bread. Two glasses of wine. Piece of chocolate.	Salmon and veggie stir-fry. Glass of wine.	Large jacket potato and tuna with salad.

Food changes to make

Things to avoid altogether
Stop having bread and butter with meals.
Stop having biscuits mid-morning.

Things to reduce
Have one teaspoon of sugar in coffee instead of two.
Limit alcohol units to seven a week, only drink at weekends.
Reduce portion size of lasagne but have more salad.

Things to replace with a lower calorie alternative
Swap semi-skimmed milk to skimmed milk.
Buy low-fat hummus.

Ways to reduce calorie intake

If you have dieted before, you've probably already realised how much psychology is involved in eating behaviour, convincing yourself you've eaten less than you have or exercised more than you have, persuading yourself that, 'The biscuits are low calorie so I can have two', or that an extra bread roll with butter won't matter. Your behaviour determines the success or failure of your diet plan. Let's face it, you know what you should eat in order to lose weight, it is doing it that is the problem.

Most of us are regularly seduced by the smell, sight and taste of food, causing us to overeat throughout the day. Research shows that we eat more in the following circumstances:

- When we are eating lots of different foods in one meal, especially at buffets or when more than one course is consumed.

- When we are doing something else while we eat, such as watching television.

* If we eat quickly.

* If we use larger sized plates which require a greater amount of food to look like a 'plateful' of food.

How many of these circumstances apply to you? Do you eat on the go or while watching television? Do you scoff food down quickly and then find yourself looking around for something else to eat? Check out the size of the plates and dishes you use at home – are they larger than other crockery sets you have?

It may be that you don't need to change the types of food you eat at all, but addressing the way that you eat will enable you to lose weight, and making adjustments to both areas of your eating behaviour will pay dividends.

Change how you eat, not what you eat!

* Keep tempting foods out of sight! Each time you see the biscuits or chocolate, you will be tempted to eat them. Store foods like this in cupboards that you don't often use. Out of sight, out of mind!

* Eat light at night. The later you eat in the evening and the bigger the meal, the less likely you are to use up the calories you've eaten. However, if you tend to snack later on after eating an early dinner, actually eating dinner later on in the evening may reduce your overall calorie intake if it stops you snacking later on.

* Get the family involved. If others in the household are eating a healthier diet with you, it becomes easier for you to stick to it.

* Eat more often, but reduce the amount that you eat at meal times. Snack on low-calorie fruit or raw vegetables.

* Drink plenty of water throughout the day so that you don't mistake thirst for hunger.

Eating out

Many people find it relatively easy to eat healthily at home but encounter calorie control problems when they eat out. Ideally, you should be able to relax and enjoy a meal out, choosing to eat whatever you want to. However, the effects of social eating upon your overall calorie intake will begin to have a detrimental effect upon your energy balance equation if this is a regular event.

Trying to opt for lower calorie options or eat healthily when eating out can be very difficult, as you are basing your decisions upon the menu descriptions, and there are two problems with this:

* A dish can sound healthy or low calorie, but when it arrives it may be covered in a high-fat/high-calorie sauce or dressing.

* Chefs want their food to taste good – and fats are laden with flavour, so it is highly likely that most restaurants will use a good deal more butter, oil, cheese and other fats in their dishes than you would use at home.

Of course, you can always follow well-known diet mantras for limiting the calorie damage of eating out:

* Drink still or sparking water instead of juice or alcohol.

* Order salads but hold the dressing or put it on the side.

* Avoid snacking on bar and table appetizers such as salted nuts and breadsticks.

* Ignore the bread basket.

* Choose soups based upon broths or vegetables rather than cream-based soups.

* Choose low-fat vegetarian, fish or lean meat options.

* Question the waiting staff so that you can make an informed choice of what to eat. Don't be afraid to ask if the chef can modify your meal to suit you by serving sauces and dressings on the side, not adding cheese to a dish, or cream to a dessert.

Additionally, if you eat out quite regularly, and/or want to be more careful with calorie intake when you eat out, see if any of these tips help:

- Don't feel left out when friends are ordering dessert – order a coffee instead so you have something in front of you to enjoy while they're piling on the calories.

- Share a pudding. Many people feel the need to finish a meal with something sweet – halve the dessert and halve the calories. You'll be doing your pudding partner a favour too.

- Don't starve yourself all day if you're going out for dinner. We are more likely to overeat and choose high-fat, high-sugar and higher-calorie foods when we're hungry, making it easy to wipe out the calorie deficit you've created during the day.

- Don't be afraid to order a starter to eat as a main meal. We really don't need to consume the amount of food that three courses provide, and often order a starter, a main meal and a dessert out of habit or to fit in with what everybody else is doing. Some menus offer starters as a small or main meal, and if you like the sound of a starter option more than any of the main meals, this is the perfect option for you. Alternatively, you could order a second starter in place of a main meal.

'Drink less alcohol – it contains almost as many calories as fat!'

Alcohol

Alcohol can be the ruin of many a good diet. As it comes in liquid form, we often don't consider its calorific value directly compared to foods, but pure alcohol provides seven calories per gram – which is just a little less than fats. As a liquid, it's also easy to consume a large volume of it without feeling full, so a couple of glasses of wine in the evenings could be the make or break of your weight loss goals.

But as with any aspect of your diet, you don't need to cut it out completely, unless you want to. Here are some suggestions to help you cut down the amount of alcohol in your diet:

- Spritzers last longer than just wine and water down your calorie consumption.

- Alternate alcoholic drinks with mineral water to halve the calories.

- Swap your wine for an alcohol-free (lower calorie) wine, or try red or white grape juice which can be diluted down with water to reduce calorie intake even further.

- Arrive fashionably late and miss the first round, and if you are drinking at home, start later! If you have made a large dint in a bottle of wine by the time you eat dinner, the wine doesn't last through the meal and you'll end up opening a second bottle.

- Don't go out thirsty – the first couple of drinks won't touch the sides! Drink lots of water throughout the day to avoid trying to quench a thirst with the first drinks of the evening.

- Offer to drive.

- Decide to stay within a certain number of alcohol units each week. Work out how many alcohol units you usually drink, then reduce it. Remember, although it depends upon the alcohol volume of each type of drink, a unit is generally half a pint of standard strength beer, lager or cider, or a measure of spirits, and a glass of wine is usually two units. It is recommended that women don't exceed 14 units a week and men stay below 21 units for good health, so these are good guidelines to start with if you're currently drinking more than this.

- Have alcohol free days, which is good for the liver too.

Start as you mean to go on

Much of the success of any diet plan comes from being organised and from controlling what is available to eat. Many people comment that they would find it easy to diet if they had a chef producing their food for them – in other words, if you didn't have to make the decisions of what food to buy and cook, and didn't have to 'run the gauntlet' of avoiding tasty treats in the kitchen, life would be so much easier. This is why meal replacement diets work for some people – the food choices, decisions and temptations are taken away. But you can gain greater control over what you eat – it just takes a little planning.

Be prepared and take control

- Plan your meals in advance for the week so you know what you will be eating and nothing is left to chance.

- Make a supermarket shopping list and stick to it.

- Don't go shopping if you are hungry. With a low blood sugar level, you will fill your trolley with sugary, refined carbohydrate foods that you wouldn't usually choose, and you know once you've bought them, you'll eat them.

- Avoid the supermarket aisles which only contain foods you are trying to avoid, so that means ignoring the confectionery and biscuit aisles. The added bonus is that you can reduce the time it takes to do your food shopping.

- Go shopping with a friend or partner who has your best interests at heart – they can step in when your willpower slips.

- If temptation is too much, get someone else to shop for you.

- Shop online where you can't see tempting food that you should be avoiding, smell the fresh bread or be drawn into buying two for one.

Summing Up

Okay, so you've bought the food and planned your meals for the week – now you just need to stick to the plan. As long as the meal planning and food shopping have been done with care, you are over halfway there.

- Stick to the meals you planned to eat through the week.

- Keep a food diary to check on everything that passes your lips. This is a useful tool to look back over, especially if you fail to achieve the weight loss goals you set for yourself.

- Make small changes to your diet that you can stick to.

- Employ a mixture of 'cut out', 'reduce' and 'swap to' dietary adjustments.

- Think about changes you need to make to how you eat, not just what you eat.

- Employ damage limitation when eating out.

- Be organised. Good organisation with food shopping, meal planning and cooking will pay dividends.

Chapter Five

Calories – To Count or Not To Count?

Many long-term dieters will have counted calories at some point, and a lot of well-known diet plans are based upon calorie content. There's no getting away from the fact that it is your calorie intake compared with your calorie expenditure that governs your body weight and the amount of body fat you store. However, counting calories can be confusing and time-consuming work. Let's take a look at what a calorie is and consider the pros and cons of counting calories in order to lose weight.

What is a calorie?

A calorie is the amount of energy required to raise the temperature of 1g of water by 1°c. It is the energy currency we use in our bodies – we take food in, break it down, store it and use it for energy. The word 'calorie' should be spelt with a capital 'C', and is actually an interchangeable term used instead of 'kilocalorie', which is equal to 1,000 calories, but the word calorie is so widely used (without the capital 'C') that we generally only see the term 'kilocalorie' on food labels and nutrition charts. The term 'kilojoules' is also increasingly used as a food energy measurement; one kilocalorie (calorie) is equal to approximately 4.2 kilojoules.

The energy balance equation

Weight control is based on something called the energy balance equation as shown below.

When energy in = energy out, weight maintenance is achieved.

So, if we take in more calories than we use up, we gain weight, and if our calorie intake is lower than our expenditure, we lose weight. If your weight has been stable for a while, this means you have achieved calorie balance; you are consuming the same number of calories as you are using up. Weight gain indicates that you have been taking in more calories than you need or are not using up as many calories as you need to.

It's a balancing act

You can either reduce your calorie intake or increase your activity levels to lose weight – or, for quicker results, do both. Although calorie counting works for some, not everyone needs to meticulously monitor their energy intake.

If you make a few changes in your usual diet to reduce calorie intake and/or do more exercise, you will lose weight, and this can easily be monitored with regular weight loss measurements. It sounds simple, doesn't it? It is quite simplistic, but there are many things that affect our food choices and activity levels, and we are also very good at tricking ourselves into thinking we have eaten less and exercised more than we actually have. Take a look at these common pitfalls that are detrimental to your weight loss efforts.

- Following restrictive diet plans that cannot be maintained for more than a few days – this leads to gorging on foods that you are craving.

- Following diets that are too low in calories, leading to low blood sugar levels and higher intakes of food at the next meal.

- Not keeping a food diary and forgetting snacks and drinks that have been consumed (a glass of wine, a few chips off someone else's plate or a handful of crisps).

- Convincing yourself that you have been more active than you really have been, or that you'll go to the gym tomorrow instead.

So, although the energy balance equation is simple and effective, actually creating a calorie deficit without measuring it can be a little tricky. In order to create a calorie deficit, it helps to have a bit more information, such as knowing:

- Approximately how many calories we need each day.

- Which foods or drinks are high in calories.

- How the activity we do each day affects our calorie balance.

Basal metabolic rate

Your basal metabolic rate (BMR) is the number of calories you need each day at complete rest – as soon as you get out of bed or eat anything, your caloric needs increase. If you are quite active, you will require more calories; you can take this into account after you have worked out the basic number of calories you need each day.

Although it is too time consuming for most of us to weigh the food that we eat and count calories with every meal, it's worth knowing how many calories your body needs each day, as it's a common error to reduce calorie intake too much. Remember though, this is just a guideline – the number of calories you need is also affected by your height, the amount of muscle you have and your activity levels.

Calculating your basal metabolic rate

- First of all, find your age range in the tables (male or female) overleaf.

- Now multiply your weight in kilograms by the figure shown for your age.

- Finally, add on the number at the end.

Female

Age	Basal metabolic rate	Your basal metabolic rate
10-17	Weight in kg x 13.4 + 692	
18-29	Weight in kg x 14.8 + 487	
30-59	Weight in kg x 8.3 + 846	
60-74	Weight in kg x 9.2 + 687	
75 +	Weight in kg x 9.8 + 624	

© Crown copyright. Source: Department of Health.

Male

Age	Basal metabolic rate	Your basal metabolic rate
10-17	Weight in kg x 17.7 + 657	
18-29	Weight in kg x 15.1 + 692	
30-59	Weight in kg x 11.5 + 873	
60-74	Weight in kg x 11.9 + 700	
75 +	Weight in kg x 8.4 + 821	

© Crown copyright. Source: Department of Health.

'Remember that your BMR is the number of calories you need at your current weight for weight maintenance. If you want to lose weight, you will need to consume fewer calories than this.'

Extra calories for activity and exercise

You can multiply your BMR by 1.4 to take account of activity during the day. Most of us would not need to adjust our calorie requirement by any more than this, although those doing regular high-intensity exercise such as running four or five times weekly might multiply their figure by 1.6 or even 1.8. However, these calculations are based upon active exercisers, and it's also worth mentioning here that most of us overestimate the amount of activity we do, so it's unlikely that you will need to adjust your BMR at all if you want to lose weight.

Don't over do it

It is a common error to reduce calorie intake too low. This is sometimes done in order to lose weight more quickly and also when weight loss has stalled, but if you reduce your calorie intake to less than your BMR (the amount of energy your body needs to function at rest) for too long, you are likely to store more fat, and muscle is used for energy. This decreases your BMR and so reduces the number of calories used over a 24-hour period – this is bad news if you want to lose weight, as you want your BMR to be higher, not lower.

However, it's worth remembering that because your calorie requirements are based upon your current body weight, as you lose weight you require fewer calories as it is easier to move a lighter body around. This is one of the key reasons for the well-known weight loss plateau – we fail to continually adjust our calorie intake as we lose weight. Of course, you can't keep on reducing your calorie intake as the body needs a certain amount of energy and nutrients to function (your BMR), but this is where regular exercise comes in.

The pros and cons of calorie counting

The benefit of calorie counting is that if you get it right, you really should be able to control your weight. However, accurate calorie counting requires:

- That you know how many calories you need to consume daily for health, based upon your height, age and current weight.

- Portion sizes and weights of food to be accurate.

- The correct brand of food to be looked up or input if using books or websites to calculate your calorie intake.

- All food and drinks consumed to be included in your calorie counting (in other words, you have to be honest).

Over time, many people get to know which foods are low and high in calories, and can make educated choices about which foods to eat based upon this knowledge. However, calorie counting can be very time consuming, especially if you are being accurate.

Don't believe everything you read

But it's not only your nutrient intake you need to worry about, food marketing can be very deceptive, and some so-called 'low calorie' or 'low-fat' foods might not be all they seem. If you rely on food labelling to provide you with accurate information, you have to learn to read between the lines. If fat content is reduced, taste is often affected, so many food manufacturers will add in sugar, salt, sweeteners or flavourings to provide additional flavour. This means that to choose a low fat but healthy food, you need to check the ingredients list and sugar and salt content as well as fat grams.

Lite or light

'It's worth considering that not all low calorie foods are good for you, and not all high calorie foods are bad for you.'

To use the term 'reduced calorie' on a food, it must contain 25% fewer calories than the standard version.

The word 'light' (sometimes spelt as 'lite') suggests that a food may be lower in calories or fat. To use this term, the food product must be at least 30% lower than other standard products in at least one nutrient or value listed on the nutrition label (for example, lower in fats, sugar or calories) and should also state which nutrient it is lower in.

In order to check this out, get used to looking at the 100g list on nutrition labels – this lists how many grams of protein, carbohydrate, fat, fibre and salt per 100g a product contains. As most food products show this information, you can easily compare one product with another. To see if a product really is lower in fat or calories, compare it with a standard product – you may be shocked to find that some 'light' or 'reduced-calorie' options are:

- Barely lower in fat and/or calories than other products.

- May be lower in fat but the added sugar to add taste has increased the calorie count so that it is no longer a low-calorie option.

- Lower in calories or fat than the same brand's standard version, but if the standard version has very high calories or fat, the 'light' version may not be that low in calories or fat when compared with another brand.

Have a look at this example of a food label to identify what to look out for:

Try to ignore the marketing

Long list of ingredients? Put it back on the shelf

The biggest ingredients are shown first

Watch out for lots of additives

Low-calorie reduced-fat cake
Scrumptious reduced-fat chocolate cake.

Ingredients
Sugar, glucose, invert sugar syrup, thickener, white flour, sucrose, maltose, hydrogenated vegetable fat, flavourings, salt, chocolate powder, regulators, E102, E110, E128, E150b, E211, E420, maize starch, colourings, stabilizers, fructose, honey, trans fatty acids, cream, egg powder.

Typical nutritional values

	Per 100g	Per 20g serving
Energy	800kcals	120kcals
Protein	3g	0.5g
Carbohydrates (of which are sugars)	70g 65g	10g 9.75g
Fats (of which are saturated fat)	27g 25g	4g 3.75g
Dietary fibre	0.1g	Trace
Salt	3.5g	0.5g

What proportion of carbohydrates are sugars?

Check how much fat is in your food

Check how big a serving is

Daily salt intake should not exceed 6g

Remember the three golden rules when reading food labels:

- Ignore the food marketing (or at least be suspicious!)
- Read the ingredients list to see what's in your food.
- Check the nutrition chart for actual grams of fats and sugars.

What is a serving size?

It's also worth checking out the 'calories per serving' information which is shown on some low-calorie products. The question is, 'How big is a serving?' If nutritional information per serving size is shown on a food product, the manufacturer must state what a serving size is. On low-calorie products, you will often find that the serving size is extremely small – so unless you consume only the amount given as a serving size, you won't benefit from the low-calorie intake. For example, a 30g serving of cereal may contain approximately 100 calories, but if you are serving yourself 100g, you are eating over three times the number of calories you may think you are eating.

Low-fat products

Many diet products will state that they are low in fat; as fats contain nine calories per gram, the amount of fat in a product is often reduced in order to lower calorie value. A high-fat product contains more than 20g of fat per 100g; a low-fat product contains 3g or less fat per 100g. It can be misleading when products such as mayonnaise which are naturally high in fat are labelled as 'reduced fat' or 'reduced calorie'. Although the fat content may be reduced, the product itself is still classed as a high-fat food. Take a look at this example of mayonnaise – the overall fat content is greatly reduced, but the actual fat content of 28.1g/100g means this is still a high-fat product.

'Take care when using "reduced fat" products – they may have a reduced fat content, but could still be high in fat and calories.'

Nutrient content	Calories per 100g	Fat content (g/100g)	Sugar content (g/100g)	Sodium (g/100g)
Normal mayonnaise	724	79.3	0.1	0.24
Low-fat mayonnaise	288	28.1	4.6	0.94

Some products based upon fats, such as margarines, may market information such as 'low in saturated fats'. If you want to reduce your intake of saturated fat for health reasons, then this is useful, but all fats, regardless of whether they are saturated, polyunsaturated or monounsaturated are all nine calories per gram, so swapping one type of fat for another will not reduce overall calorie intake. Watch out for this claim on sauces and dressings too.

The downside of low-calorie processed foods

When we eat reduced-calorie foods, we often give ourselves license to eat more because it is lower in calories, often eating so much more that we end up consuming the same number of calories we would have eaten had we consumed the 'full-fat' or normal option.

One problem with many low-calorie foods is that they aren't very filling, and we are likely to eat more of them in order to feel full. Because we are used to a certain level of fullness, we continue to eat until we experience that feeling, which often leads us to consume the same number of calories as normal, even when consuming low-calorie foods. Fruits and vegetables naturally get around this problem because of their high fibre content. Fibre makes us feel full, providing the satisfaction that isn't found with reduced-calorie products, although some 'diet foods' now have added fibre to help overcome this and fill you up, which may contribute to part of a healthy, balanced diet.

Calorie counting versus eating a healthy diet

Another problem with very low-calorie diets is that the fewer calories you consume, the more difficult it becomes to take in enough of the essential nutrients required for good health – vitamin and minerals, for example. So, it's important to ensure that your diet contains nutrient-dense foods if you are reducing your overall calorie intake. If calorie counting is the only factor that you consider when making food choices, this can sometimes lead to a less than healthy diet, particularly if you have a penchant for biscuits and cakes! There is a wide range of low-calorie foods to choose from, but unfortunately, rather than change our diet to one packed with naturally low-calorie fruit and vegetables, it can be too tempting to rely upon processed foods labelled as low-calorie to determine our energy intake. These foods are often highly processed and contain very little nutritional value.

So although there are some benefits to counting calories, there are also several considerations, particularly when designing a long-term healthy eating plan. Try to judge a food on its overall merits, considering whether it is healthy and nutritious as well as how many calories it contains.

'Following a healthy diet should involve widening the range of foods that you eat, not reducing it.'

Summing Up

Counting calories is just one way to lose weight and maintain a healthy body weight. However, for a healthy, long-term eating regime, use the information from this chapter to fine tune calorie counting:

- Always consider the energy balance equation.

- Calculate your BMR to see how many calories you need.

- Don't reduce calorie intake below your BMR.

- Read between the lines on food labels.

- Make sure low-calorie or low-fat foods are still healthy options.

- Consider the overall nutrition of foods as well as the calorie content – remember, foods with a high protein or fibre content will fill you up and help to prevent overeating and snacking.

Chapter Six

Portion Size – Just as Much to Blame!

One thing that many of us need to pay more attention to is the amount of food that we eat, rather than the type of food, which is where most dietary attention is focused. You can gain weight due to an excess calorie intake from any type of food, not just high-calorie or fatty foods. So if you think your diet is healthy, but you struggle to lose or maintain a healthy weight, portion size may be to blame.

Surrounded by temptation

We are constantly bombarded by larger portions of food than we actually need:

- 'Two for one' offers in the supermarket.
- 'All you can eat' buffets at restaurants.
- Large portion sizes when you eat out.
- Large portion sizes at home.
- Large portion sizes when eating out at friends' houses.

These larger food portions are seen as a bargain, a bonus, good value or generosity. We don't stop to consider the fact that we don't need, or even really want, the additional food, and once it is bought into the home, or placed upon a plate in front of us, we are extremely likely to consume it.

A study on portion size and calorie intake carried out by Kral *et al.* (2004) showed that we will automatically eat more food if it is given to us, but we still feel satisfied with smaller portions when this is all that is provided. This indicates that we are eating past fullness when a greater amount of food or food of higher calorie density is provided.

'If you consume more calories than you use up, you will gain weight. It's as simple as that!'

What happens to the extra food?

Our body can only metabolise so much food in one go, whether we eat carbohydrates (rice, pasta, vegetables), protein foods (meat, fish, eggs) or fats (cream, butter, oils).

Carbohydrates and proteins have many useful roles in the body, but excess that cannot be used (or stored, in the case of carbohydrates) may be converted into fat and stored as body fat. So you could be eating a fat-free diet and still lay down excess body fat if you eat too much carbohydrate or protein. Alcohol follows the same fate: once metabolised in the liver, if it isn't used up for energy, it may be stored as body fat. Some fats have useful roles in the body, but any excess will be stored as body fat, and much of the saturated fat we eat, which has fewer useful roles in the body, will be stored.

'A good rule to follow for healthy weight maintenance is to eat until you are 80% full.'

How much is too much?

Protein foods are filling, so we are less likely to over eat these foods. However, carbohydrates, which are digested more quickly, are a different matter. Large servings of cereals, potatoes, pasta and rice are common, and although these are generally healthy foods, consuming too much in one meal increases the likelihood of the excess carbohydrate being converted into fat and stored. For example, a large 100g portion of cereal may provide approximately 290 calories (without any milk, sugar, yoghurt or fruit added). A 40g portion, which is a reasonable portion size, provides 116 calories. Making this change would result in you consuming over 1,000 fewer calories weekly – a substantial cut in your energy intake!

However, breakfast should be sustaining enough to provide energy through to lunchtime to prevent snacking on sugary foods, so reduce your portion sizes slowly and snack on fruit, raw vegetables or rice cakes mid-morning if you get hungry. It's worth checking out portion sizes of other commonly eaten carbohydrates too.

- A large (125g, uncooked) serving of pasta could weigh in at 440 calories (without the sauce), but a 50g serving provides 176 calories – a saving of 264 extra calories every time you eat pasta.

- A large (100g, uncooked) serving of rice could weigh in at 358 calories (without any sauce), but a 50g serving provides 179 calories – a saving of 179 extra calories every time you eat rice.

So it's easy to see where those extra calories may be coming from if your portion sizes are a little too large, a little too often! Making changes like this could have a significant effect on your overall calorie intake.

Breaking a bad habit

Pouring a certain amount of cereal into a bowl every morning, or preparing a certain amount of vegetables for an evening meal, is a habit that means you could be consistently preparing more food than you need. Once food is prepared or cooked, it is highly likely that you will consume it all. If your food tastes nice, you will want to finish your meal, regardless of whether you feel full or not, and there is also pressure not to waste food and throw it away. Can you see how one action (preparing too much food) is causing another action (having to eat the food)? The same happens when we go food shopping – if you buy more food than you need, you are much more likely to eat it once it is in the house.

The good news is that simply pouring out less cereal, or peeling fewer vegetables, is somewhat 'removed' from the actual eating process and is easier to change than trying to exert the will power to stop yourself eating something. If you simply weigh out or prepare less food, you will eat less food. However, you may still need a few tips to help you, as there is going to be less food – or certainly fewer calories – on your plate.

How to eat less food

Your stomach is an elastic sac which expands to accommodate the amount of food eaten. In addition to other mechanisms which help to control when and how much we eat, there are stretch receptors in the walls of the stomach. As the stomach enlarges with food and stretches, these receptors send a message back to the brain telling us to stop eating. The sensation we feel is known as satiety – the feeling of fullness. However, most of us ignore this feeling if there is still food on our plate and we are enjoying the food. The amount of food we eat and the level of fullness we are used to is habitual, so in order to get past this monumental barrier to weight loss, you will need to know:

- How to cope with eating less food than you are used to.
- How to respond to the satiety message your body is giving you.

How to cope with eating less food than you are used to

'Missing meals or cutting calorie intake too low is a false economy... you will just overeat at the next meal and over-compensate for the calorie deficit you created earlier.'

One thing that contributes to our feeling of fullness is the amount of food on our plate. A fuller plate is less likely to leave us feeling hungry, even if the calorie density is not as high as in a smaller meal. In order to avoid feeling 'short changed', you need to make smaller food portions look like a 'normal' plate full. Here are some tips to help.

- Use smaller plates and dishes so that you don't feel 'cheated' from the outset and do feel like you have had a plate full of food.
- Complement your dish with high fibre, lower calorie, less starchy fruit or vegetables. You can gradually reduce the amount of starch-rich pasta, potato, rice or cereal portion of your meal, but fill it out a little with fruit or vegetables which are higher in fibre and lower in calories. This will help to fill up your plate or dish and increase the size of your meal while reducing calories.
- By eating regularly you will stabilise your blood sugar levels and avoid overeating. If you are over-hungry when you begin a meal, you will eat at a faster rate. The faster you eat, the more likely you are to finish your meal before your stomach has chance to send the fullness message.
- Eat slowly. This gives your body a chance to recognise that you are full and should stop eating! Many of us have already finished our meal before this 'message' is sent! The chances are that if you eat slowly enough, you will feel full before you finish your plateful and will not want a bigger portion anyway.

64

- Sipping water between mouthfuls can help to slow down the pace of your eating.

- Doing something else while we eat, like watching TV, takes attention away from our meal, making us more likely to eat quickly and not notice how much we have consumed. Sit down at the table and be mindful of the food you are eating – enjoy and savour it!

How to respond to the satiety message our body is giving us

- Listen to your body. When you begin to feel full, stop eating.

- Get used to leaving the last couple of mouthfuls on your plate.

- Throw leftovers away immediately so that you don't starting eating them later, but note how much food is left as this is the additional amount of food you have prepared in error. Next time you have this meal, reduce your portion size by this amount to avoid wasted food and temptation to finish the plate.

- Instead of having another serving, refrigerate or freeze left over food for another meal.

Reducing the calorie content of your meal without reducing meal size

Having a full plate or dish of food in front of you will help you psychologically so that you don't feel like you are 'on a diet', but there are additional benefits to making these dietary changes. As well as being lower in calories, fruits and vegetables tend to contain a very wide range of nutrients such as vitamins, minerals and phytonutrients (plant nutrients that are known to enhance good health). What tends to happen when we are dieting is that as we reduce the amount and range of food we eat, our intake of essential nutrients also reduces, so finding ways to add back in nutrient-dense foods such as these is a bonus. Fruits and vegetables also contain high levels of fibre and water, both essential nutrients that help to reduce calorie intake while simultaneously enhancing health. It is the high fibre and water content of these foods that give them a low-calorie density, as there are no calories in water and very few in fibre, but these nutrients increase the volume of food, helping us to feel full.

What to reduce	What to add in
Reduce your portion size of breakfast cereal	Add any type of fruit – berries, citrus fruits, apple, pear, melon, apricot and mango all work well.
Reduce your portion of rice	You can add vegetables to the rice while it cooks, risotto-style. Pack it out with onions, garlic, frozen peas, peppers and sweetcorn. Alternatively, cook the rice separately but add extra vegetables to the other part of your meal, packing out chilli, curry or stroganoff with nutrient-dense, low-calorie vegetables.
Reduce your portion of pasta	Replace starchy pasta with water-rich aubergines, courgettes, red onions and tomatoes for a lower calorie and tastier Mediterranean style meal with added health benefits.
Have fewer potatoes	Swap potatoes for other vegetables. The bright colours of vegetables such as pumpkin, carrot, beetroot or broccoli denotes the high levels of phytonutrients in these foods, which all contain less starch and fewer calories than potatoes.
Make an omelette with one less egg and less/no cheese	Add in tomatoes, peppers and onion to fill out the omelette.

You could reduce the amount of fish or meat you have on your plate in favour of lower-calorie vegetables; however, protein-rich foods like meat and fish make us feel full for longer, so the reduced-calorie intake could be short lived if you begin to feel hungry again soon after your meal.

Important note for foodies

Remember, you are replacing one type of food for another – not simply adding fruit and vegetables to your meals! The plan is to reduce your overall calorie intake, not increase it. If you serve your usual portion of porridge and add fruit to it, this will increase your nutrient intake but also add to your calorie intake. You have to reduce your portion size of starchy carbohydrates and add some fruits and vegetables to the meal to replace the starchy carbohydrates removed. Don't go mad and add five tablespoons of different berries to your cereal, or six different vegetables to your pasta (unless in very small amounts). When we add several foods to a meal, it can be easy to end up with too much on the plate.

Everything in moderation

Although eating a wider range of foods is better for us, it is a common error when preparing food to cook or prepare a serving size of each food to be eaten, regardless of how many foods are in the meal. A meal of meat, potatoes and peas has three components, whereas a meal of meat, potatoes, peas, carrots and broccoli has five components, so the portions of each, or at least some, should be lower. However, when preparing food we tend to visualise a 'serving size' of each component on the plate, regardless of how many components are in the meal. If you are preparing a meal with more components to it, you must reduce the amounts of each food in order to limit the overall calorie content.

What is a portion size?

A portion size is approximately the size of the palm of your hand, but how many 'portions' should you have in a meal? A healthy, balanced meal would include the following:

- One portion of protein food (such as fish, eggs, meat or beans).

- One portion of starchy carbohydrates (such as rice, pasta, potato or beans).

- Two portions of fruits or vegetables.

The eatwell plate opposite illustrates the healthy balance of foods in your overall diet. Using an image like this can help you to visualise how to keep your overall calorie intake under control. It's also a good idea to change what you eat, so don't constantly leave out the starchy carbohydrates altogether, as these foods do provide some nutrients that fruits and vegetables are not so rich in. Don't forget that your protein portion (meat, fish, eggs) is likely to contain quite a high amount of fat, so this is another food group you might pay attention to when considering portion sizes. Variety is the key to good health.

The eatwell plate shows how much of what you eat should from each food group. This includes everything you eat during the day, including snacks. So, try to eat:

- Plenty of fruit and vegetables.

- Moderate amounts of bread, rice, potatoes, pasta and other starchy foods – choose wholegrain varieties whenever you can.

- Some milk and dairy foods.

- Some meat, fish, eggs, beans and other non-dairy sources of protein.

- Just a small amount of foods and drinks high in fat and/or sugar.

But keep portion sizes small!

The eatwell plate

Use the eatwell plate to help you get the balance right. It shows how much of what you eat should come from each food group.

Bread, rice, potatoes, pasta and other starchy foods

Milk and dairy foods

Foods and drinks high in fat and/or sugar

Meat, fish, eggs, beans and other non-dairy sources of protein

Fruit and vegetables

A diverse diet – the pros and cons

Eating a wide range of foods at each meal is beneficial for good health, but you will have to run the gauntlet of calorie control at every meal. When we are presented with a greater variety of foods, although the range of nutrients is enhanced, the likelihood that we will overeat is higher. This is because a range of different food flavours and textures encourages us to eat more; we are less likely to become bored with one type of food and we ignore the feeling of fullness. This is experienced when eating out – we may feel 'full' and would not choose to order another plate of lasagne, for example, but will gladly consume a dessert.

Therefore, when replacing some of your calorie-rich foods with other foods, here are some guidelines to ensure that you still succeed in reducing your calorie intake:

- Don't add too many different foods to a meal – if you are replacing some of your starchy carbohydrates with fruit or vegetables, just add a small amount of each fruit or vegetable; if you are replacing a starchy carbohydrate in a meal completely, replace it with two portions of fruits or vegetables.

- To really ensure you get it right, weigh your foods. If you are reducing your cereal portion by 25g, just add 25g of fruit. If you are reducing your rice portion by 50g, add 50g of vegetables. As fruits and vegetables have a much lower carbohydrate content and a much higher water content, they contain fewer calories even though you are replacing the carbohydrates with the same weight of fruits and vegetables.

In fact, fruit and vegetables have such a high water content (for example, raw carrots are 89% water weight), you can add even more of these non-starch polysaccharides (fruits and vegetables) and still create a calorie deficit.

The table opposite shows the water, fibre, nutrient and calorie content of three fruits or vegetables that you could use to replace some of the starchy cereal, rice or potatoes in a meal. There are no calories in water, so the greater the water content of food, the lower the calorie content is. All foods are uncooked so you can compare the calorie content of 100g of rice with carrots, 100g of oats compared with blackberries and 100g of potatoes compared with broccoli.

You can see that because fruits and vegetables contain so much water and fibre, you could add double the weight of these foods to the amount of starchy carbohydrate you have removed from your meal and still have a lower calorie intake. For example, if you reduce your rice portion by 50g, you save 191.5 calories, and even if you add 100g of carrots (rather than the 50g of food removed), you only gain back 35 calories, giving you a saving of 156.5 calories.

	Water weight (g)	Protein (g) (4 calories per gram)	Fat (g) (9 calories per gram)	Carbo-hydrates (g) (4 calories per gram)	Fibre (g)	Overall calories per 100g
White rice	11.4	7.3	3.6	85.8	0.4	383
Carrots	89.8	0.6	0.3	7.9	2.4	35
Ready Brek	8.3	11.6	8.3	65.4	8.0	366
Blackberries	85	0.9	0.2	5.1	3.1	25
Potatoes	79	2.1	0.2	17.2	1.3	75
Broccoli	88.2	4.4	0.9	1.8	2.6	33

All figures are for 100g uncooked foods.

(Source: statistics are sourced from the Food Standards Agency, 2002. © Crown copyright.)

Remember, rice and pasta should be weighed before cooking as they absorb so much water during the cooking process.

Summing Up

Portion size is the root of the problem for many dieters, and as calorie counters will know, it's not what you eat, it's how much you eat that matters. Having said this, filling up on lower calorie fresh foods is a much healthier option than limiting dietary intake to a few mouthfuls of ice cream and chocolate.

For a weight loss plan that works for life, keep an eye on your portion sizes.

- Prepare less food to begin with – you can always have a snack later if you haven't had enough to eat, but if you prepare too much, it's likely you will eat it whether you need it or not.

- Fill up your plate with lower calorie foods such as vegetables – the increased size of the meal will make you feel fuller.

- Eat slowly – and stop eating once you feel full.

- Remember, satiety is specific to the food you feel 'full' from eating – a smorgasbord of food will result in a higher calorie intake.

Chapter Seven

Weight Loss through Exercise

Weight loss is most successful when healthy eating is combined with regular exercise. The great thing about being reasonably active is that as well as keeping you fit and healthy, it allows you to indulge on the food side of things a little bit more. However, if the very mention of exercise has you breaking out in a cold sweat, the likelihood is that you've just not found an activity that suits you yet. Let's explore how you can lose weight by using up more calories through activity and exercise.

This chapter is for you if:

- You find it difficult to find ways to reduce your current calorie consumption.

- You would prefer to keep some 'treats' in your weekly diet and use activity and exercise to create a calorie deficit.

- You want quicker results by reducing calorie intake and increasing calorie expenditure.

There are many ways of using up more calories throughout the week. Regular exercise is the best way to use up energy, but increasing your activity throughout the day can also help. Even if you exercised for an hour daily, there are still another 23 hours in each day (15 if you deduct eight hours for sleeping) during which you can help yourself to lose weight. Here are some ways in which you could fit extra activity into your daily routine. As with the tips to reduce calories, choose the options which will suit you the most, as you'll be more likely to stick with them.

Fitting more activity into your life

- Use the stairs rather than the lift – especially if you work or live somewhere with stairs and can make this a regular calorie burner.

- Don't send emails to office colleagues – bring back the art of conversation and walk to their desk to give them a message.

- Don't drive around car parks until a space right next to the door is free – park further away and walk. Even better, leave the car at home.

- Get off the bus, tube or train a stop early.

- Walk the children to school.

- Walk to the shops instead of sending someone else or using the car.

- Take up an active hobby such as dancing or gardening.

- Take the dog (or other people's dogs) for a walk.

- Don't put the housework off – it may be boring, but vacuuming, dusting and even ironing can all notch up reasonable calorie expenditure.

'Keep an activity log with your food diary. Jot down every extra activity you do each day. This will motivate you to try to do something extra every day, just so you can write it down.'

Exercise

Nothing can beat the benefits of regular exercise for reducing body fat levels and helping you to maintain a healthy body weight. Although many people begin exercising to lose weight, if you choose an exercise that you enjoy, you'll feel healthier and fitter, and also enjoy the social benefits that many types of exercise offer. Weight loss often just becomes an added bonus.

How much exercise do I have to do?

If you plan to lose 1lb a week, you need to create a calorie deficit of approximately 500 calories a day – but how long would you need to exercise to do this? It depends on how much effort you put in and which type of exercise you choose to do. The more effort you put in, the more calories you use up, so you can exercise for a shorter period of time if you are prepared to work harder.

For example, you would need to walk at a fast pace for almost two hours to use up approximately 500 calories, but you could use up the same amount of calories in a 45 minute run.

Of course, the amount of calories you use up is individual; your weight, body composition and fitness level all affect how much energy you utilise. But as a guideline, here are some other examples of workouts that would use up approximately 500 calories.

- 45 minutes on a step machine in the gym.

- Just over an hour playing a reasonably hard game of tennis.

- 3-4 hours of golf (without the buggy).

- One hour of cycling.

How hard to I need to work?

Most of us exercise well within our comfort zone at a level that feels comfortable, without getting out of breath or sweating too much. However, this fails to give us a 'training effect'. Scales of perceived exertion can be used to determine the intensity level of exercise (how hard someone is working). On a scale of 1-10 of perceived exertion, we often remain below six. To really make a difference, you should exercise at a rate of perceived exertion (RPE) of seven or eight.

The 'talk test' is used in the health and fitness industry to help exercisers measure their exercise intensity level. If you can have a full conversation with someone without getting breathless, you're unlikely to be exercising at a high enough intensity to create a training effect – you're taking it easy! However, you should be able to speak a sentence or two – if you can't say anything, your intensity level is too high to be maintained for long, certainly not throughout an endurance activity such as swimming or running.

It is essential that you continue to push yourself as you become fitter and lose weight. As your body becomes used to the exercise, the activity becomes easier to do. This accustomisation, combined with any weight loss, means that you are using fewer calories during the same workout and the exercise

'To make exercise effective, you should feel slightly out of breath and be able to speak a sentence but not have a conversation.'

will begin to contribute less to your weight loss goal. Exercising for longer, changing the exercise session or increasing the intensity will ensure that the exercise you do remains effective.

How long do I need to exercise for?

The American College of Sports Medicine is an authority on the effects and benefits of exercise. Their recommendation for all healthy adults is as follows:

- Do aerobic exercise 3-5 days per week
- Exercise at 55%-90% of your maximum heart rate.
- Exercise for 20-60 minutes.

The longer you exercise for, the more calories you will use up. As we use up our limited amount of stored carbohydrate energy, we begin to use more body fat as fuel instead, so exercising for longer results in more body fat being used up. For exercise sessions longer than 40 minutes duration, work out at a medium intensity to maximise fat-burning potential. If you have less than 40 minutes available for a workout, you will need to exercise at a higher intensity to use up the same number of calories. Try to exercise at a RPE of eight.

So, the less time you have available to exercise, the harder you'll have to work to burn the same amount of calories.

What type of exercise is best?

Cardiovascular exercise

Cardiovascular, or aerobic, exercise is any activity that makes the heart and lungs work harder – the type of activity that involves large body movements and gets you out of breath. Here are some examples of popular cardiovascular exercise:

- Walking and power walking.
- Jogging and running.

- Swimming.
- Cycling.
- Fitness classes.
- Dance classes.
- Rowing.
- Step and cross training machines.
- Wii Fit activities.

As cardiovascular exercise uses large muscle groups, this is the type of exercise that uses more calories, so you need to include some types of cardiovascular exercise in a weight loss routine every week.

Weight-bearing exercise burns more calories

Although any type of exercise is a good thing, there are some types of exercise that are better than others as far as calorie expenditure is concerned. These tend to be the higher intensity cardiovascular exercises such as running, where you are supporting your body weight. For example, cycling and rowing are classed as non-weight-bearing exercises because your body weight is supported by a seat. Although these types of exercise are still beneficial, you have to work harder at them to use up the same number of calories you would expend in a weight-bearing exercise over the same length of time. When you are swimming, your body weight is supported by the buoyancy of the water, making this a non-weight-bearing exercise. However, you do have to propel yourself forwards through the water, so this helps to increase the intensity of the exercise.

Take a look at the chart overleaf which gives approximate calorie expenditure per hour for various activities. The weight-bearing activities shown in the shaded boxes use up more calories than the non-weight-bearing types of exercise.

'Weight-bearing exercises such as walking, running or aerobic fitness classes will use more calories than seated exercises such as rowing or cycling at the same intensity and duration, as you are carrying your body weight at the same time as exercising.'

Activity	Approximate calories/hour
Running (7.5 miles per hour)	697
High impact aerobics	414
Rowing at moderate intensity	365
Cycling (10 miles per hour)	305
Swimming (recreational)	250

(Source: www.weightlossresources.co.uk.)

This doesn't mean that you shouldn't swim, cycle or row, it just means that you have to work harder at these activities, or do them for longer, to make them as effective as weight-bearing activities.

High impact versus low impact exercise

High impact exercises are those where both feet are off the ground at the same time, as in running and high impact aerobics, whereas low impact activities always have one foot on the ground, for example during walking. Low impact exercises tend to be lower intensity than high impact activities, but some low impact activities can still be weight bearing and of a high intensity, such as power yoga, hill walking and weight training.

Weight training

Although you may be seated during many weight training exercises in the gym, it is considered a weight-bearing exercise because of the resistance applied against each muscle worked. This, combined with the training effects of weight training, make the gym a good option for weight loss.

It is a common perception that weight training will increase body weight. However, although weight training may increase the amount of muscle you have, and may therefore increase your overall body weight by a little, the overall effect will reduce body fat levels. This is because the more muscle you

'For every extra pound of muscle you put on, your body uses around 50 extra calories a day. In a recent study, researchers found that regular weight training boosts basal metabolic rate by about 15%. This is because muscle is "metabolically active" and burns more calories than other body tissue even when you're not moving.'

Juliette Kellow, Weight Loss Resources.

have, the higher your metabolic rate is. This means that you will use up more calories, whatever you are doing, over a 24-hour period. Gaining muscle helps to turn your body into a fat-burning machine!

Unless you follow a body building routine lifting heavy weights, you won't build large muscles, and most weight training programmes will tone up the muscle that you have, tightening and shaping your body. This in itself will make you look and feel slimmer, so it's a good idea to include one or two weight training sessions a week in your fat loss exercise programme in conjunction with some calorie-burning cardiovascular exercise.

The best exercise for weight loss

Interval training is very effective for weight loss – this is when you work hard for a set time (for example, one minute), then exercise at a lower intensity for a minute (you can alter the timings). Working harder for short spurts enables you to exercise harder than you usually would, as you only stay at this level for a short period of time. During the higher intensity phases you use up more calories than normal, but the lower intensity phases (when you return to your 'normal' exercise intensity level) allow you to recover. Doing an entire workout at the higher intensity level is unrealistic, but adding spurts of higher intensity will burn more calories and increase your fitness levels. You can incorporate interval training into many different types of exercise:

- Jogging – jog for a minute then walk for a minute. As you become fitter, increase the time you spend jogging and decrease the time you spend walking.

- Cycling – cycle at a faster speed for two minutes, then slow down for a minute. As you become fitter, increase the faster cycling time or add in some hills which also heighten intensity.

- Swimming – swim one length quickly then swim back at your normal pace. Try to gradually increase the ratio in favour of faster lengths, as your body becomes accustomed to the quicker pace.

Get a pedometer

A pedometer is fixed to your waistband or belt, and counts the number of steps you walk each day. It can be a good tool to help you increase the amount of activity you do just by moving around more, and you can set yourself a daily step goal. Health experts recommend a goal of 10,000 steps each day, but if this is much more than you currently do, it may be an unrealistic target. Instead, find out how many steps you do in a typical day and then set yourself a target to increase it to (for instance a 10% increase). Once you are achieving your new target steps each day, set a new goal to increase it again.

Many pedometers, particularly less expensive ones, can be inaccurate. They may count movements such as jiggling your leg while seated. If you pay more for a quality pedometer, as well as increased accuracy, it is likely to measure other things such as distance travelled and estimated calorie expenditure. Visit www.weightlossresources.co.uk for a range of quality pedometers.

Getting started and sticking with it

It can be really difficult to begin – and stick with – a regular exercise regime. How many times have you begun to exercise and then stopped – or maybe never got started in the first place? However, there are a number of psychological tools you can use to create a regular exercise habit and achieve your weight loss goal.

Dissociation

For many people, being out of breath, feeling hot and sweaty and exercising at a high intensity is not an enjoyable experience, and the only way to get through it is by doing something that takes your mind off exercise. This is called exercise dissociation. Take a look at these common ways of 'switching off':

- Listening to music while you exercise.
- Watching TV or listening to music in a gym.
- Chatting with a friend while you exercise.

'Up to 80% of people do not have the "self management" skills to continue with regular exercise without some sort of support system, explaining why many of us stop and start exercise many times over the years.'

* Concentrating your mind on something else while you exercise – revision, work problems, reading the paper, etc.

Dissociation takes your mind off the exercise you are doing and relieves boredom and exercise discomfort.

Exercising with others

One of the most successful ways to stick with regular exercise is to exercise with other people. This is for a number of reasons:

* It can take your mind off the exercise.

* It can relieve boredom.

* It can make the exercise more enjoyable and sociable.

* You are less likely to miss an exercise session if you are letting someone else down.

* There may be an element of friendly competition.

* A bit of morale support helps.

Enjoy exercise

It is essential that you find something that you enjoy doing – if you don't enjoy it, you won't keep it up. There are many different reasons for exercising, which can be split into extrinsic and intrinsic factors. Tick off any of the examples on the table overleaf to help you decide whether your exercise motivations are, or have been, intrinsic or extrinsic.

The difference is that extrinsic factors are less likely to help us stick with exercise in the long run. If you exercise because you feel you have to, ought to or should do, this is shaky ground for a long-term exercise habit. If, however, you exercise because you enjoy it, or you like the way regular exercise makes you feel, these intrinsic factors are linked with a healthy, long-term exercise habit which will support long-term weight loss.

'Some research has shown that 90% of us prefer to exercise with others, and we are up to 22% less likely to stop exercising if we exercise with other people.'

Intrinsic (you gain satisfaction from exercising itself)

I enjoy the way regular exercise makes me feel ☐

Regular exercise makes me feel healthier ☐

Exercise energises me ☐

Extrinsic (you are exercising for a benefit other than the exercise itself; for example, to lose weight)

I need to exercise to lose weight ☐

I have to exercise to look better ☐

I should start running to get in better shape ☐

How will I know what type of exercise I enjoy?

In the same way that we choose our hobbies or careers, there is an activity or type of exercise out there for everyone, you just need to figure out what suits you! You may need to think back to the last time you exercised regularly (which might have been at school) and try to remember what activities you enjoyed. Was it team sports, competitive sport or activities where you could push yourself?

Various studies have linked exercise success to different personality traits – if you choose a type of exercise that suits your personality, you're more likely to enjoy it, and if you enjoy it, you'll stick with it. See if you can spot your personality and then try out the suggested activities for your type.

Spot yourself...	Try one of these...
Competitive	Squash. Tennis. 10 km competition runs. Triathlons.
Sociable	Fitness classes (anything from yoga to aerobics). Running or walking clubs. Get involved in a squash or tennis league. Swimming clubs or aqua aerobics.
Self motivated	Go to the gym and set weekly goals. Running, cycling or walking alone. You'll be able to go swimming and just complete lengths of the pool.
You have a sense of adventure	Mountain biking. Water sports. Hill walking. Diving – join your local sub aqua club.
Do you have an aggressive nature or need to let off steam?	Boxercise classes (boxing fitness). Kickboxing or other martial arts. Circuit training. Running.

The most important thing is that you enjoy what you're doing, so try a few different things and see what works for you.

Finding time to exercise

The factor quoted most frequently as a reason for not exercising is lack of time. Exercise takes a back seat to almost everything else in most people's lives, but we often over-estimate how much time is needed to fit in an exercise regime that will make a difference. Remember, every bit counts – even if you only exercise for 20 minutes, it might use up an extra 100 calories, will increase your metabolic rate for a while and help you to get into the habit of exercising.

Think about when you could exercise:

- An early workout before breakfast.
- During the day.
- In a lunch break.
- After work in the evening.
- At the weekend.

Although this may seem fairly obvious, it's worth taking time to plan when you will exercise and organising your day around it. Write it in your diary or on the calendar and begin to book other things around the exercise, rather than trying to fit exercise in around everything else.

Benefits of an early morning workout

- Working out first thing means that regardless of how your day turns out, you have already exercised. This is a good option if you have a busy schedule, or if you are likely to put off exercise.
- Early morning exercise is a great energiser, setting you up in a great frame of mind for the rest of the day, and can help you to stick to your healthy eating plans.
- Early morning exercise can be an effective 'fat burning' workout as you will have less stored carbohydrate available and will use more fat for fuel.

'Having an "all or nothing" attitude to exercise often results in "nothing" being done. If you haven't got enough time for a one hour workout, just do two shorter workouts!'

Lunchtime exercise benefits

▨ Research shows that exercise at lunchtime improves focus, concentration and effectiveness during the afternoon when energy and concentration levels usually drop.

▨ The sociable aspect of exercising with work colleagues will increase your enjoyment of exercise, and once you're in the habit of going to the gym at lunchtime, you are likely to stick with it.

▨ Exercising during the day gets the workout done before you relax at home in the evening, when it is notoriously difficult to find motivation to go and exercise.

Exercising in the evening

▨ Early evening is the time when our cardiovascular efficiency and muscle strength are at their highest, making 4pm to 6pm the most effective time for exercise.

▨ You are less likely to have pressing engagements that limit exercise time, so you can spend longer exercising if you want to.

Weekends and days off are typically a time when, although there is more time for exercise, the time is often spent doing other things. Try to do different types of activity with friends or family which will help you to use up more energy.

▨ Go for a walk.

▨ Go swimming.

▨ Go cycling.

▨ Do an activity such as horse riding or ice skating.

▨ Play tennis or badminton with family or friends.

▨ Have a Wii Fit party.

Goal setting

Setting exercise goals can also help you to stick with regular exercise, and can be a better type of goal than a weight loss goal. Weight loss goals are based upon body measurements, which can be unpredictable and demotivating when we don't get the results we want. However, if we measure the exercise we do in order to lose weight, we have more control over the outcome and are likely to be more motivated by the results along the way.

For example, you might decide that you will exercise twice weekly. Note down your exercise sessions as you do them and tick off that achievement at the end of the month. An even better goal is to plan a set number of workouts per month so that you can play 'catch up' in case you miss a workout, and the goal is not lost immediately. Planning to complete a set number of exercise minutes is even better, and your goal should be based upon current activity levels and realistic aims, but also pushing yourself a little.

Get a personal trainer

If all else fails and you simply can't motivate yourself to exercise regularly, why not get a personal trainer? It is less expensive if you buy sessions in packages of 10 or more, and having one session weekly may motivate you to exercise on your own or with a friend between sessions. Plus, you'll have the benefit of having a professional who will note measurements, help you to set goals and monitor your progress in addition to getting the very most out of you in each exercise session!

'Measuring weight loss is an outcome goal based upon the results of weeks of dieting and exercise, whereas measuring the amount of exercise done is a process goal. For increased success, measure the journey rather than the outcome.'

Summing Up

So, taking all that into account, a successful exercise plan for weight loss will look like this:

- Choose a type of exercise that you enjoy.

- Unless you are self motivated, plan how you can exercise with a friend or group.

- Set yourself an exercise goal that you will measure in 4-6 weeks' time.

- Choose weight-bearing and higher intensity activities that will use up more calories.

- Try to add some spurts of higher intensity into your exercise session, and keep your overall RPE above six (see page 75).

If you're really keen to lose weight, reducing your calorie intake and increasing your calorie expenditure will obviously create a bigger calorie deficit, as you take in less and use up more energy. Just make sure you're eating enough to provide energy for your exercise sessions!

Chapter Eight

Weight Loss Tools and Gimmicks

In an industry said to be worth £10 billion a year in the UK and $40 billion in the US, anything that may help you to lose weight is big business. The latest diets, must-do fat-burning exercises and diet pills and potions are constantly being marketed to us with weight loss promises designed to make you buy them. Many of these products promise fast weight loss with very little effort required on your part. Sounds too good to be true doesn't it? The problem is, it usually is.

Although there are numerous anecdotal accounts of successful weight loss for many of these weight loss products, actual clinical research showing definite reductions in weight are often few and far between. Even if a 'fat magnet' herb or appetite suppressant helps you to lose weight, are you going to take this product for life? What happens when you stop taking it?

Weight loss products may be based upon reducing your appetite, blocking the absorption of nutrients like fat in the digestive tract or raising your metabolic rate with ingredients such as caffeine. While these ideas would, in theory, aid weight loss, we need to consider how they work, whether there are any side effects and if there is a placebo effect. Most products suggest that a calorie controlled diet should be followed at the same time, and some offer an exercise challenge to take part in. So what is really causing the weight loss?

However, there are also several helpful tools available which can aid weight loss, and these are the effective groups and programmes that have been formed to support lifestyle changes.

'Ironically, when we buy a weight loss product, this is often when we make additional efforts to change our diet and lifestyle, which means you are not measuring the success of the weight loss product alone.'

Weight loss groups

The weight loss group has proved to be an effective and enjoyable way to lose weight for many people. Most weight loss groups combine reduced-calorie eating programmes with a weekly weigh in and encourage regular exercise. Information, group discussion and peer support form a part of the weekly meetings, creating a social and supportive environment. Most large-scale weight loss groups also offer an online option if you are unable to get to the group meetings – information on how to find your local group or join online can be found in the help list.

Online weight loss resources

With our increasing reliance upon web-based amenities and information, online resources can offer an informative, interactive and effective way to help you lose weight. As long as the advice is sound and the website easy and fun to use, this could form the backbone of the guidance and support you need to help you lose weight and maintain a healthy diet. As with local slimming groups, there is a charge to join most of these weight loss websites, but some offer a free trial or free use of some of the tools or information on offer.

There are many such websites, so how do you know which one to trust? Check out the list below as a guide of what to look for.

- Information and advice from qualified nutritionists or dietitians.
- Healthy, balanced meal plans providing a wide range of foods and adequate calorie intake.
- BMI or waist circumference calculators to help you know how much weight you need to lose.
- Suggested weight loss goals are within 2lb per week (unless you are very obese in which case initial weight loss can be more).
- Calorie counters for individual foods and meals.
- Options to keep a food diary and exercise log online or in a diary.
- Recommendations and ideas to increase your activity levels.

With tonal work we divide the page into areas of grey shade. Therefore we do not distinguish individual objects, but rather the shapes and gradation of tone.

These are two purist extremes. What tends to happen in most drawing is a mixture of both. We observe the outline and filling in the tone.

To add to this our brains are very good at shape recognition. That is taking recorded experience and mixing it with the visual information available. Much of the time as artists we struggle against this. We try only to observe what is actually before us.

This may sound odd, but most people don't actually see what is really there. It is much more efficient to take key points from the reflected light and let our brain fill in the rest. We make assumptions based on experience. So when we say the primary skill of drawing is learning to look, it means learning not to make assumptions about what we perceive. Being an artist is about seeing the world differently from the majority of other people, because we are actually seeing it.

Obviously learning to discard or limit a natural process is difficult, and most drawing exercises are designed to train us in this.

The actual marks made in an image are, if you'll excuse the pun, just surface detail. If we start to find a certain style or technique attractive there is a danger that our marks will become vain. They'll start to pout and flirt with our eyes and distract from the actual observation. Changing the way we work can not only help guard against this danger but also, because we may require different information to describe it, change the way we look at an object.

There are many reasons for approaching still life. Some incline towards the training aspects, a bridge between, or solid base for other art. Some wish only for the solitary meditation such studies bring, others approach still life for still life's sake. What we wish to gain should inform how we adapt and approach the exercises that follow. We should always try to establish the point of what we are attempting. This gives us both direction and a criteria to assess how successful we have been. Being able to analyze our own work and see its strengths and weaknesses is probably as hard to learn as drawing.

There is so much more to say about mark making and drawing and the philosophy of different approaches. For example; when our marks go beyond observation and attempt to encompasses emotions; or the balance between how much should be drawn and how much not drawn. However these discoveries and ideas are best made through actually doing. Let's get it on!

THE BASICS

WHERE, WHAT?

So where are we? It could be that after buying this book we decided to go to a cafe, or maybe we are now sitting at the kitchen table. Let's get something to drink, and while we are doing so, grab a pen and some paper. It doesn't really matter whether it is lined, squared or plain and a biro or some equivalent will suit our purpose.

So what are we waiting for? Our subject now sits cooling before us. So before we enjoy our drink let us sketch it. We should try to draw the essence of our object and not become caught up in detail. Simple clean lines are best, but if we do linger on some detail that's not a problem. The key to success in art is enjoying what we do and doing it some more.

SHOPLIFTING

There is great wisdom in the saying "set a thief to catch a thief". The more thoroughly we understand our own trade the more able we are to observe our peers.

Can we see anything wrong with the sketch above? Initially it is an impressive study of some shopping. If we look more closely however we start to notice subtle errors. It's

strength is in surface detail, it's weakness is in the objects form. It has not been drawn all at once and so has become unbalanced.

Take the partially obscured can of baked beans. If the ellipses had been initially worked out then the details would not struggle against the form, they would reinforce it.

The HP bottle to the left shows a lack of attention compared with the

details lavished upon other items.

It is much easier to notice these things in the drawings of others or with the distance that time brings to our own work.

This highlights the benefits of working with other artists or with putting our work aside and returning to it later. Nothing we ever do will be all bad or all good.

AN AID TO PLOTTING

Throughout time artists have developed various methods to help study proportions. Probably the most well known method is a system of visual measuring using an outstretched arm and a drawing implement. We all know that the further away something is the smaller it appears. With the arm at full extension the hand's distance from the eye remains constant. We can then measure the relative heights of objects and the distance between them in terms of, for this example, brush heads. The total height of the mug is about one and a half heads, the nearest apple is about half. The same apple is about one head higher than the base of the cup, and so we construct our image with relative measurements.

A plumb line is a simple device, often a weighted piece of string, that can be hung central to our composition - vertically dissecting it. Taking a straight edge we can then judge the important angles and plot invisible lines in relation to our constant plumb line.

In diagram 2 we can see how simple our plumb line is in relation to the chaotic arrangement of objects. For further clarity we can take a straight edge and hold it so that it joins the objects. Then judge the angles in relation to our plumb line. In the lower part of the diagram the image has been faded and the invisible lines drawn in.

EASIER STILL

Getting progressively more technical we have the gridding method. Taking a piece of stiff card we cut a central hole proportional to our canvas. Then with careful measurement we evenly divide the central space with stretched wire or string. This grid can then be held before our still life. Our paper should also lightly gridded, to proportionally match that of our card.

Diagram 4 shows our still life as viewed through the grid neatly divided into bite size pieces. Like, for example the grey bordered piece below. Obviously it is much easier to see things broken into smaller simple parts.

These methods have been created to aid our spatial judgement, not as a replacement. We should think of them much like the stabilizing wheels we use when we are learning to ride a bicycle. With practice we can discard them. Again the more we practice the sooner this will be.

WALKING THE LINE

A criticism that could be aimed at the drawings so far is their lack of spontaneity. They have all been very precise and controlled. In the interest of balance it is time to loosen up.

Drawing circles and ellipses is a good way to loosen our wrists and gain control over these simple forms. Changing our approach to drawing requires a more philosophical outlook. Paul Klee was once described by his students as 'The Buddha of the Bauhaus'. Although Klee's published writings can be hard to negotiate, his drawings and approach have inspired a great many artists. "Taking a line for a walk" is probable Klee's most well known quote and style of working.

Using a non-erasable drawing tool demands commitment to the line. Our lines should be bold and unafraid, no turning back and no erasing. So let's us set up a simple still life. Take a pen and some paper.

The first rule is that the drawing implement should not leave the surface of the paper. The main thrust of this exercise is hand eye coordination. As our eyes explore the composition before us our hand should mirror their movements with an unbroken line on the page. If our eyes suddenly flick from one side of the composition to the other then so should the line on our page.

Keeping the drawing quick will keep our lines fresh. The drawing should be infused with energy.

This is fun and as such we should enjoy it, boredom kills art.

Varying the way we approach a subject is much like drawing it from many different angles. This time however we are approaching the act of drawing in order to understand the process more thoroughly.

40

ACRYLIC STUDY

With ink washes we can only work in one direction, from light to dark. Once the wash is laid down there is no going back. If we work in oils or acrylic we can work from light to dark and back again. It is much more forgiving because if we make a mistake we can paint over it. Another advantage is that any pencil guides disappear under the first layer of paint. The above study was done with paynes grey and titanium white on cartridge paper.

73

BLOCK STUDIES

As with line work it is very beneficial to make quick studies of basic shapes. With these studies of children's blocks we can see the way light sits and is reflected over the various surfaces.

We should not be ashamed of our pencil lines. These are personal studies and not finished pieces of art. They are drawn to aid our learning process. As we become more confident we can start to use line less and less.

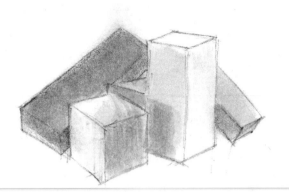

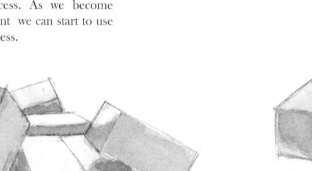

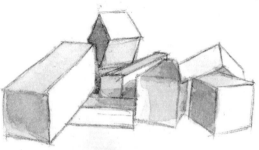

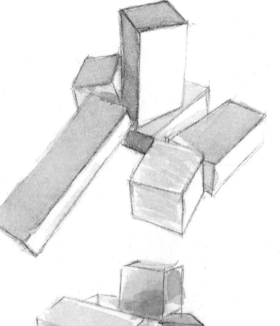

SLOWER THAN A SKETCH

As we discussed earlier, simple dark washes are quick, which is an advantage in sketching. With studies we can afford to take a little more time. With a weaker ink wash it will take longer to build up the layers, but the finished work will be more naturalistic.

CLOTH

TEXTURES IN CHARCOAL

This is a drawing of a knife handled whip with the knife removed. There are three different materials here, polished leather, fur and the battered tin blade. All have been drawn with the same simple technique using a narrow stick of charcoal. Throughout the book we have concentrated on the essential form of objects in both line and tone. Now we have the basic skills we can start to look at how to communicate surfaces and textures.

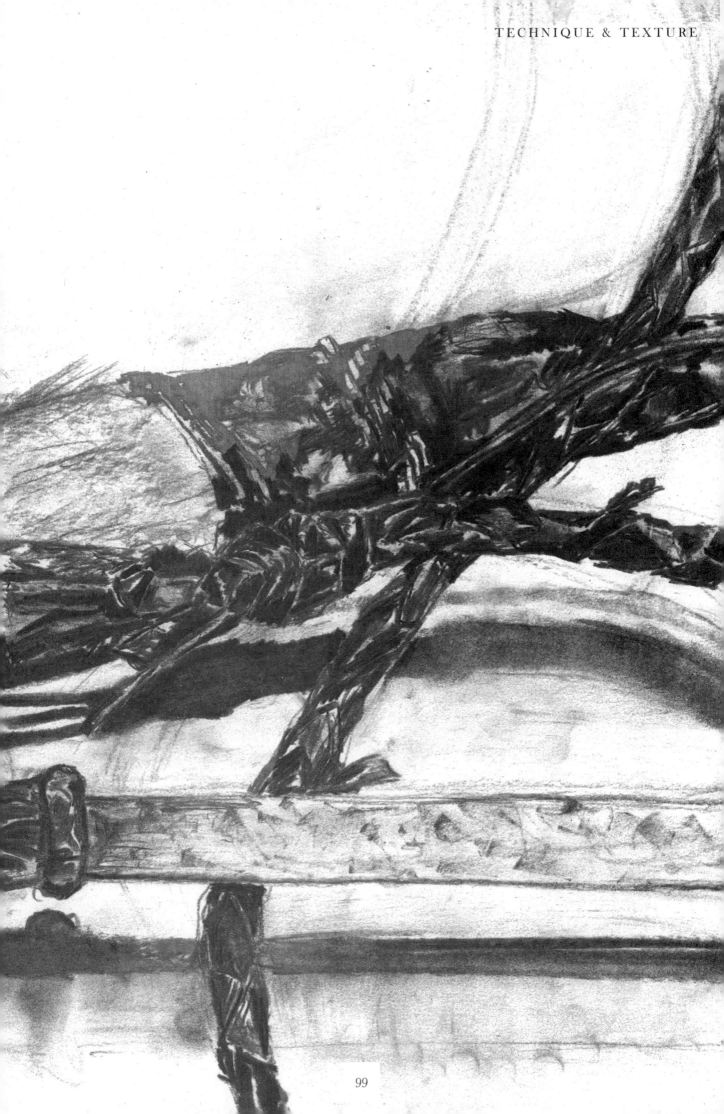

DIFFERENT STROKES

To start with it is best to choose a technique that we are most comfortable with. In this case a soft pencil, light watercolor wash and white acrylic. Then let us gather a collection of strongly textured surfaces.

On this page we start with a textured cloth and a wicker basket. Beginning with only a small section fron each, we need to find our own methods for communicating each material.

What becomes quickly apparent is that we are not trying to draw each molecule exactly as we see it. We have to extract the essence of the surface that we are drawing. This is a form of pattern making. Our marks need to assimilate and not copy what we are seeing. When we are confident that we have captured this essence we can test it by applying the surface to another object. Like for example an apple or a mug. The objective is to not let the surface destroy or distract from the form.

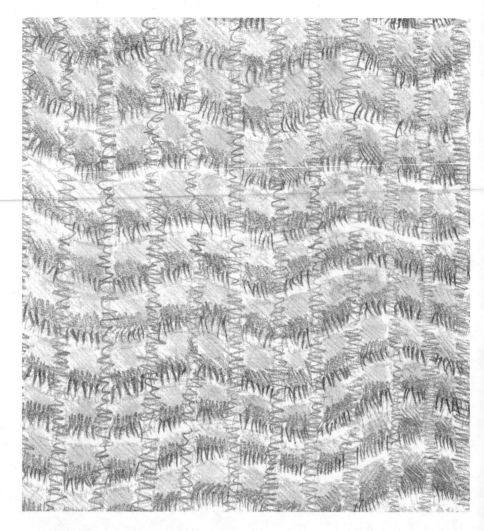

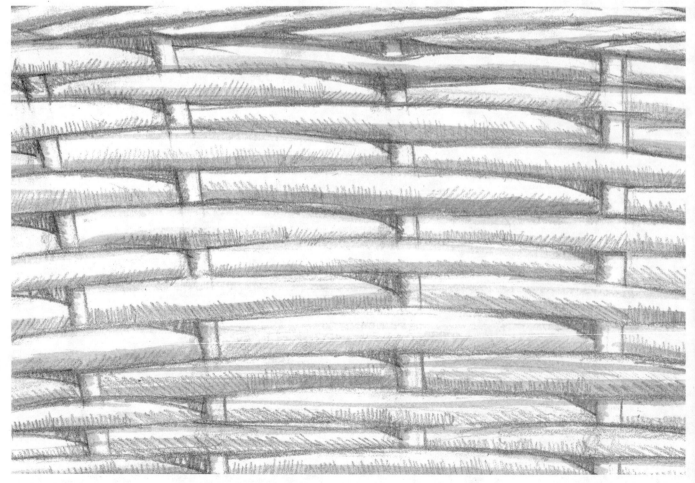

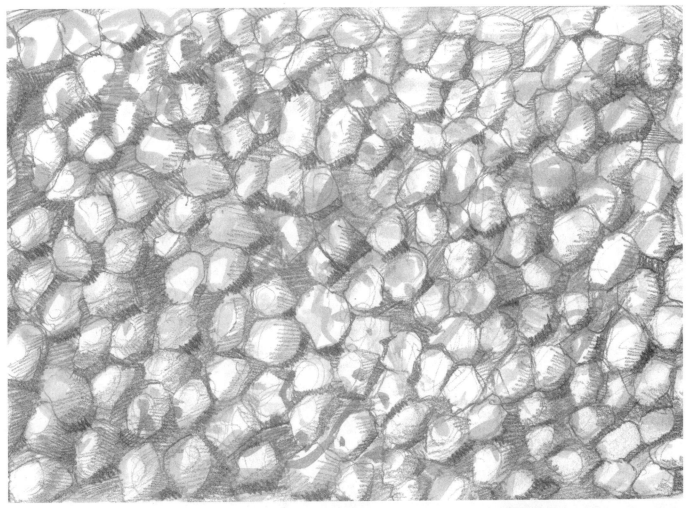

Above is a detail from a pile of stone clippings.

To the right an old piece of bark.

These exercises should be kept relatively small and once we feel we have mastered the surface move on. This sort of work has the potential to be exceptionally dull. If we start to struggle with boredom, stop and do something more interesting. We can always return to these studies at a later time.

Keep in mind that we are building up to a final piece. This work will have another dimension. Not only will it have great form, tone and technique, but also surface detail. This will complete our range of drawing skills as a still life artist.

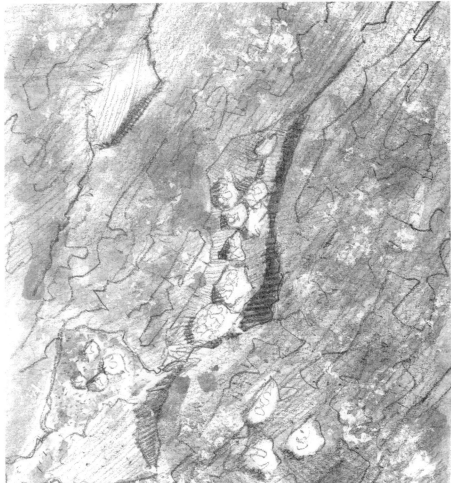

TWO TYPES OF STONE

On this page we are looking at two types of stone.

To the right we have a study of a large broken stone.

Below is a detail from a rough brick fire place.

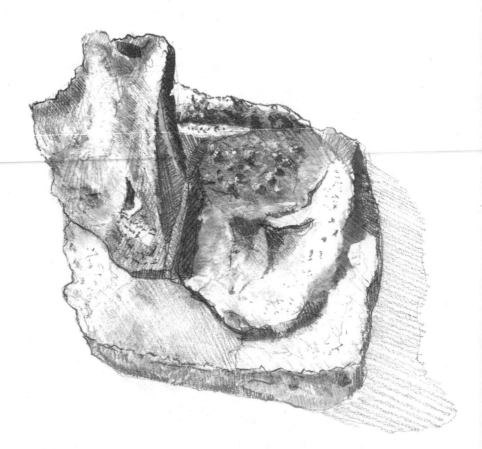

CLOTH

On the opposite page we have two studies of cloth.

The upper is a towel - this is a particularly difficult surface to capture.

The lower is the folds of some strongly lit cotton cloth.

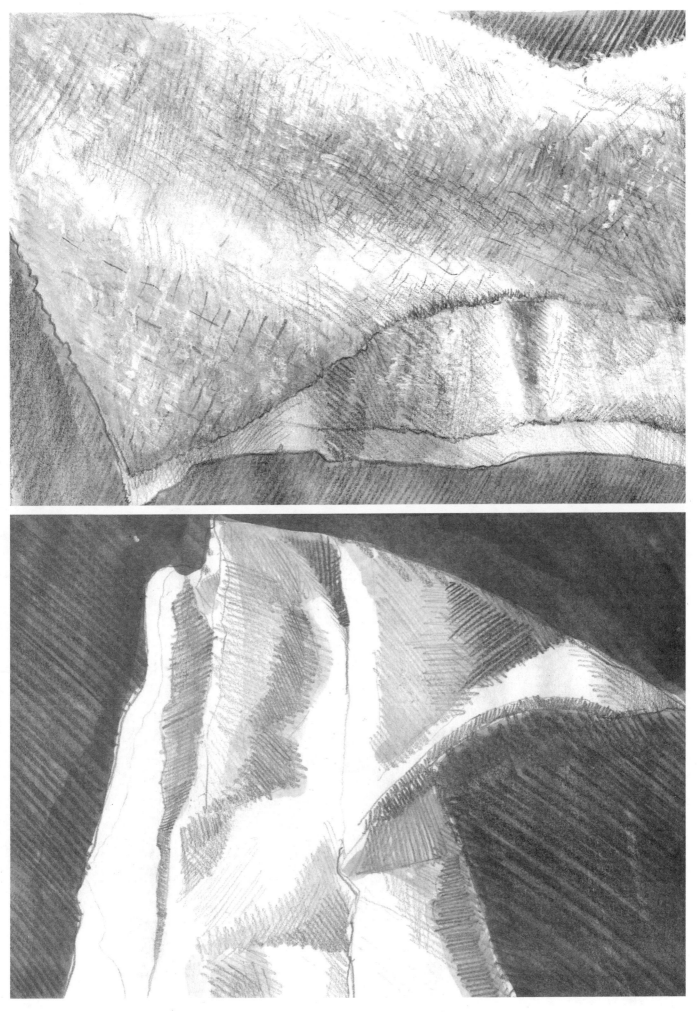

illusion of forms in space on a flat surface. Over the last few pages we have looked at different solutions to this. The theory is all well and good but is useless we are able to put it into practice. The best way we can absorb and acquire a feeling for any theory is to use it. A good way we can approach this is to break it down, work with each in isolation until we are comfortable with it. Eventually building up to subtle blend that best suits our own preferred method of work.

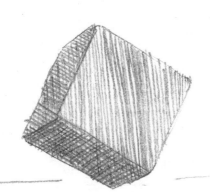

PERSPECTIVE.

To our eyes, as parallel lines move away from the central point of our vision, or recede into the distance, they taper. The point at which they finally meet is known as the vanishing point. Still life doesn't usually involve extremes of distance and so the effects of perspective are very subtle. Immediately right we have three cubes in an extreme demonstration of the distorting effects of perspective. The top cube is pulled towards a single vanishing point, hence the name one point perspective. The central cube demonstrates two point perspective. The lower cube has no parallel lines and three vanishing points. It is therefore known as three point perspective and is closest to visual reality. This said we should now be able to take the three bordered illustrations and say which is, one point, two point and three point perspective. Also we can work out where the vanishing points are by following the lines to there conclusions.

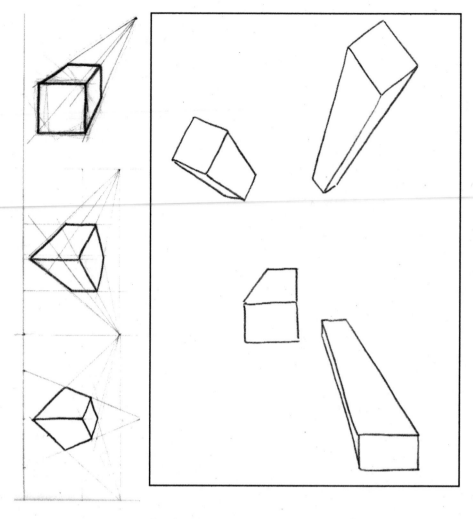

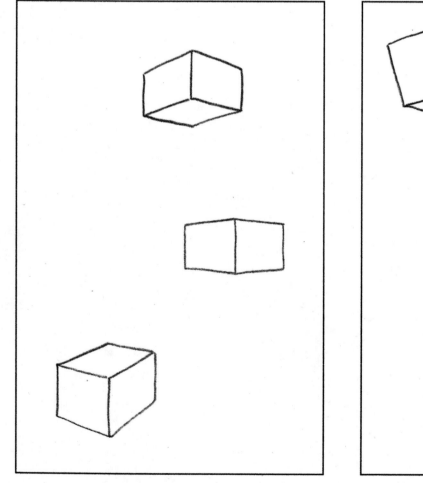

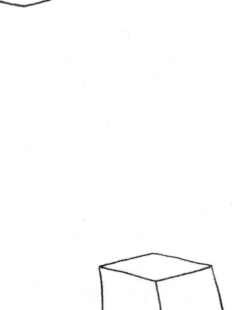

IT'S THAT EASY

Generally in still life, because of the lack of extremes, we rely on observation to inform our drawing. However understanding basic principles of perspective helps us understand, and so better perceive, what lies before us.

If the theory is so easy how is it that so many thick books have been written on the subject? What most of these books do is expand upon the principle that; 'things get smaller as they recede or move away from the centre of our vision'. The statement that parallel lines only exist as an abstract concept, is a logical conclusion based upon the core principle. Everything else follows in the manner that, if this is true, then that must be so.

For example, lets take the core principle and put it with the fact that we have two eyes. Where is the center of our vision? If we imagine a line that runs between our two pupils and a perpendicular line that crosses this in the centre, we now have the center of our vision. We also have an imaginary cross, with a vertical line and a horizontal line, to which all our vanishing point must lead. (We may already know one of these as the horizon line).

Our visual horizon line is not always the same as the line of the horizon, where sky meets land. So why is that? In the illustrations to the left we can see the varying levels of the line of the horizon when looking from above head height, waist height and foot height. When we look down on a cube we see more of the top surface than when we look at it straight on. When we look at a cube from below we see the underside. The same applies in the three illustrations, as we get lower we see less of the land and more of the sky.

In terms of our visual horizon line we cannot see the top of anything above the line and conversely we cannot see the bottom of anything below it. It is similar with the vertical line and the left and right side of an object.

Here we have four ways of laying out our compositions to see if they work, ranging from a most basic line to diagram to a fully involved sketch. Preparatory work is essential in working out the skeleton of our final image. Sketching the forms on paper to see which arrangement is most effective and pleasing. We must consider that if our prep work is too simplistic we may not get a good impression of how the final piece will look. Conversely if it is too involved we may never get round to a final piece. As in all things we must find a balance.

PLAYING WITH COMPOSITION

Let's say we need to work on a square canvas, but are struggling to get a group of objects to work in this format. Collage is a wonderful way to play with visual ideas. It is particularly strong when dealing with composition.

There are several reasons for this: Simple collage is very quick to work with; we only need to concentrate on the arrangement of the images and not on drawing them; and the images we use will often inspire their own arrangements.

When working quickly we can finish an image, decide whether we feel it has worked or not, and then move onto another. This means we can quickly get a feel for the proportions of our chosen canvas. It's possible to comfortably do over thirty images in one day, which is a lot of learning.

The fact that we do not need to concentrate on drawing the image means we can devote our attention purely to the composition. Which is obviously an advantage. Again we are removing all other distractions so that we can concentrate on our area of difficulty.

The images themselves often work best when put together in certain ways. This often leads to solutions that we would have not normally arrived at by any other method.

Practice Exam A

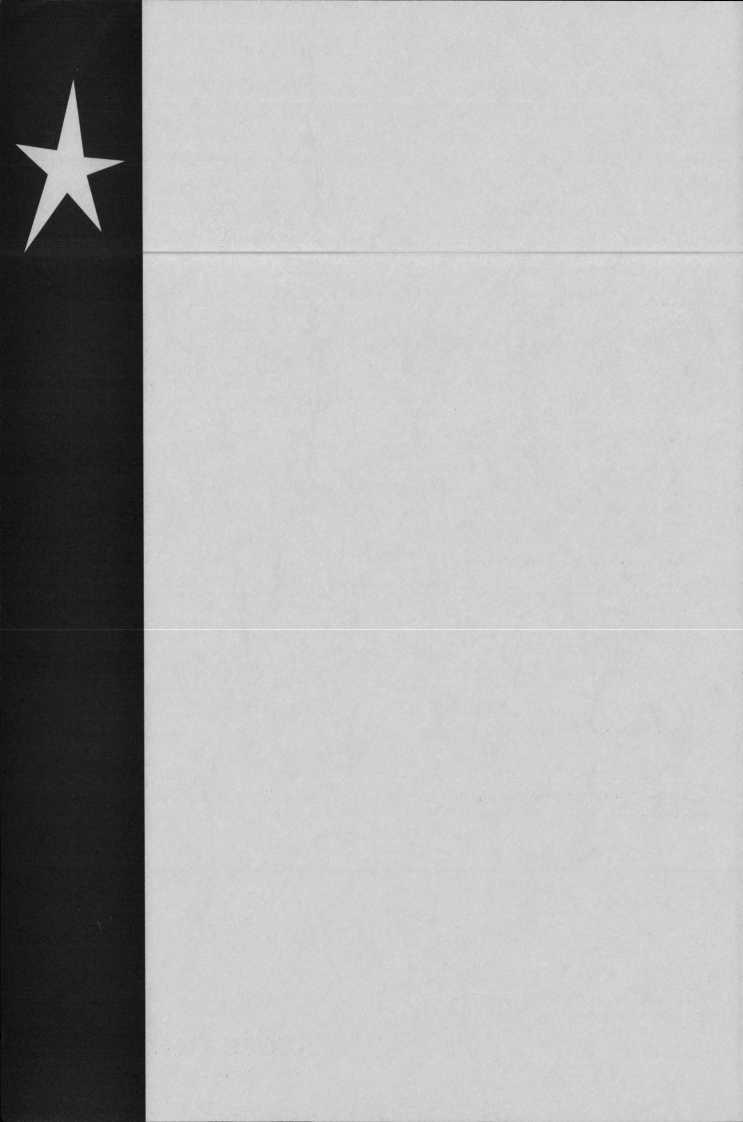

Practice Paper A: Higher English

Practice Papers
For SQA Exams

ENGLISH
HIGHER
Exam A
Close Reading

Answer all of the questions

You have 1 hour 45 minutes to complete this paper.

Read the following passages and then answer the questions. Remember to use your own words as much as possible.

The questions ask you to demonstrate that you:

understand the ideas and details in the passage – **what the writer has said**
(**U**: Understanding)

can identify the techniques the writer has used to express these ideas – **how it has been said**
(**A**: Analysis)

can comment on how effective the writer has been, using appropriate evidence from the passage – **how well it has been said**
(**E**: Evaluation)

The code letters (U, A, E) are next to each question to make sure you know the question's purpose. The number of marks per question will give you a good idea as to how long your answer should be.

Scotland's leading educational publishers

Questions on Passage 1

1. Read carefully the first sentence (lines 1–4).

    (a) What, according to the author, is the 'third certainty'? Use your own words as far as possible.   2   U

    (b) Show, by her use of language in this sentence, how the writer makes clear her disapproval of the 'third certainty'.   4   A

2. Read lines 8–15.

    What point is the writer making by her reference to the early editions of the *Encyclopaedia Britannica*?   2   U

3. What, according to the author in lines 16–18, caused the decline in the Scots language?   3   U

    Marks Code

4. (a) What point is the author making in lines 21–24 ('But we are not beyond... transactions')?   2   A

    (b) How effective is her use of imagery in making her point clear?   2   A/E

5. (a) What, in your opinion, is the structural significance of the question at the beginning of line 24?   2   A

    (b) 'Let me count the ways' (line 24). In your own words, briefly summarise the 'ways' that the writer sets out in the rest of the paragraph.   3   U

6. Read lines 50–55 (from 'Self-evidently, having a greater presence in the classroom... primacy of Irish Gaelic').

    Show how the writer's use of sentence structure supports her point that compulsion via immersion in the classroom' does not work.   2   A

7. What lesson does the writer draw from the 'Irish Board's 30-odd-year campaign to promote language in everyday life'?   1   U

8. To what extent do you find the final sentence an apt conclusion to the passage a a whole?   2   E

        (25)

Questions on Passage 2

Marks Code

9. (a) In your own words, say what it is that the writer thinks is 'extremely good for children' (lines 4)?   **2 U**

(b) Show how the writer's use of language in lines 6–12 creates a smug tone.   **2 A**

10. Read lines 13–21.

(a) 'But memorising text is only part of the process' (line 13). Explain in your own words what the writer believes to be 'considerably more important'?   **2 U**

(b) Show how the writer's use of word choice and sentence structure conveys her delight in the poetry of Burns.   **4 A**

(c) What is the writer's attitude to the bloggers, and how does her use of language draw attention to that attitude?   **3 A**

11. Show how the writer's use of anecdote in the third paragraph (lines 27–31) supports her point that much of Burns' poetry is beautiful.   **2 A/E**

12. (a) Why, according to the writer, do some critics argue that Scots does not require the same 'emergency preservation' as Gaelic?   **1 U**

(b) What do you think is meant by the term 'emergency preservation' as used by the writer in line 36?   **2 U**

13. How effectively does the last sentence (lines 43–46) conclude the ideas of the passage?   **2 E**
(20)

Questions on both Passages

14. Both passages appear to cherish the preservation of the Scots language.

Which of the two writers do you think presents the more persuasive view for preserving the Scots language?

Justify your choice by referring to the **ideas** and **style** of **both** passages.   **5 E**
(5)

Total (50)

Practice Paper B: Higher English

Practice Papers
For SQA Exams

ENGLISH
HIGHER

**Exam B
Critical Essay**

Answer two of the questions.

You have 1 hour 30 minutes to complete this paper.

You have to take each question from a different section.

You should answer TWO questions, each chosen from a different section (A-C). You must not choose both questions from the same section.

You may answer each question using texts by Scottish authors.

Make sure that you state the number of the question you are answering in the left hand margin and please take a new page for each answer.

You should divide your time equally between each essay.

The examiners are looking for evidence of the following skills:

- your ability to provide an answer relevant to the question asked and an ability to set out and develop a relevant line of thought

- your knowledge and understanding of the themes and significant, relevant aspects of the chosen texts, as well as your ability to provide detailed, supporting evidence

- your ability to show, where relevant, the ways in which writers' choices of form/structure/language can be used to shape meaning, as well as your ability to provide detailed, supporting evidence

- your ability to evaluate the effectiveness of the text, along with your ability to provide detailed, supporting evidence

- your ability to communicate clearly and accurately, using appropriate written expression.

25 marks are allocated to each question.

SECTION A – DRAMA

Answers in this section should show, where relevant, detailed understanding of the theme(s) of the chosen text and should be appropriately supported by knowledge of relevant dramatic techniques, such as – structure, setting, characterisation, dialogue (including, where relevant, soliloquy and monologue), plot, central scenes, climax, dénouement, as well as all relevant aspects of stage instructions, particularly the use of lighting, sound, stage sets...

1. Choose a play where our sympathies for the main character change during the course of the play.

   Show how the dramatist manipulates our sympathies in this way and go on to say how the changes contribute to the overall themes of the play.

2. Choose a play in which the main character is rejected or even reviled by others around him, but who is eventually respected and even admired by the end.

   Show how the dramatist makes us aware of the ways in which he is rejected and how the eventual respect that he or she earns contributes to the overall impact of the drama.

3. Choose a play where the setting is important to the overall success of the play.

   Demonstrate the importance of the setting and go on to show how it contributes to the outcome of the drama.

4. Choose a play which depends on a dramatic climax.

   Explain how the dramatist prepares us for the climax and discuss the ways in which it enhances your appreciation of the play.

SECTION B – PROSE

Prose Fiction

Answers in this section should show, where relevant, detailed understanding of the theme(s) of the chosen text and should be appropriately supported by knowledge of relevant fiction techniques, such as – narrative technique, structure, setting, characterisation, symbolism, dialogue, plot, central scenes, climax, atmosphere, imagery...

5. Choose a **novel** in which the main character(s) is (are) increasingly isolated from his or her (their) community.

   Explain briefly the causes of this isolation and go on to show the contribution such isolation makes to the overall impact of the novel.

6. Choose a **novel** where the ending raises more questions than answers.

   Explain how the novelist prepares us for the ending and go on to discuss its contribution to the novel as a whole.

7. Choose a **novel** or **short story** with dark, uncertain undertones.

   Explain the means by which the writer has created the undertones and, in more detail, discuss their contribution to the theme(s) as a whole.

8. Choose **two short stories** which approach the same theme in quite different ways.

   Demonstrate what the theme is and go on to show how their very different approaches contribute to it.

Prose Non-fiction

Answers in this section should show, where relevant, detailed understanding of the theme(s) of the chosen text and should be appropriately supported by knowledge of relevant non-fiction techniques, such as – structure (including sentence structure), narrative technique (including narrative voice), ideas, style, selection of detail, setting, symbolism, use of anecdote and/or evidence, climax, atmosphere, imagery...

9. Choose a **non-fiction** text whose theme you found moving or disturbing.

   Explain what it is about the theme that so disturbed or moved you and go on to show in more detail the means by which the writer presented this theme.

10. Chose a **non-fiction** text which is concerned with presenting a person's life story.

    Explain how the text is structured and go on to discuss the means by which the person's character is made convincing for you.

11. Choose a **non-fiction** text that deals with a foreign setting.

    Show the means by which the writer draws attention to the foreign nature of the setting and go on to discuss the contribution that setting makes to theme.

SECTION C – POETRY

Answers in this section should show, where relevant, detailed understanding of the theme(s) of the chosen poem(s) and should be appropriately supported by knowledge of relevant poetic techniques, such as – structure (including verse form, rhythm, rhyme), sound, mood, tone, contrast, setting, characterisation, symbolism, synecdoche climax, atmosphere, imagery, word choice...

12. Choose a poem which is a dramatic monologue.

Show how the poet's use of the form of the dramatic monologue reveals the gap between the impression we have of the speaker and the way in which he/she sees himself or herself.

13. Choose **two war poems** by different poets.

Compare the ways in which the poets use poetic and linguistic techniques to convey their vision of war.

14. Choose a poem which presents a likeable character.

Discuss the various means by which the character is presented.

15. Choose a poem which deals with a social theme.

Show how the poet's development of the theme leads you to a greater understanding of the issues involved.

SECTION D – FILM AND TV DRAMA

Answers in this section should show, where relevant, detailed understanding of the theme(s) of the chosen texts, and should be appropriately supported by knowledge of relevant film and TV drama techniques, such as – structure, setting, characterisation, dialogue, plot, symbolism, synecdoche, editing/montage, sound/soundtrack, mis-en-scène (such as lighting, colour, use of camera, costume, props), mood, casting, genre.

16. Choose a **film** or **TV Drama*** which has a scene where the conflict between two characters is at its most intense.

Show how the film or programme makers make clear the intensity of the conflict and go on to show how the conflict enhanced you appreciation of the text as a whole.

17. Choose a **film** or **TV Drama*** which deals with a social issue of relevant importance.

Show how the film or programme makers make clear the relevance of the issue and go on to show how your interest and emotions were engaged by the treatment of the issue.

18. Choose a **film** or **TV Drama*** in which one of the likeable characters is drawn into corruption by a society that surrounds him.

   Show how the film or programme makers make clear the nature of the corruption and go on to discuss the ways in which you remain involved in what happens to that character.

19. Choose a **film** or **TV Drama*** which captures and maintains your interest by its powerful visual impact.

   Show how the film or programme makers make clear the intensity of the visual impact and go on to show how the characters present are developed by means of the images used.

   *'TV Drama' includes a single play, a series, or a serial.

Practice Paper D: Higher English

Practice Papers For SQA Exams	ENGLISH HIGHER **Exam D** **Close Reading**

Answer all of the questions

You have 1 hour 30 minutes to complete this paper.

Read the following passage and then answer the questions. Remember to use your own words as much as possible.

The questions ask you to show that you:

understand the ideas and details in the passage – **what the writer has said**
(**U**: Understanding)

can identify the techniques the writer has used to express these ideas – **how it has been said**
(**A**: Analysis)

can comment on how effective the writer has been, using appropriate evidence from the passage – **how well it has been said**
(**E**: Evaluation)

The code letters (U, A, E) are next to each question to make sure you know the question's purpose. The number of marks per question will give you a good idea as to how long your answer should be.

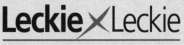
Scotland's leading educational publishers

PASSAGE 1

Rosemary Goring considers the full consequences down through the centuries of the Battle of Culloden, 1746.

FORGET CULLODEN: TODAY'S HIGHLANDERS HAVE IT MADE

1   Culloden Moor is one of the bleakest places on the planet. I know, because I've been there. Wind-blasted, sodden, as featureless as a desert, it is made even more dismal thanks to the memory of the dreadful events that took place there on April 16, 1746. In less than an hour, King George II's men
5   routed Bonnie Prince Charlie's army, and sent those who evaded capture fleeing for their lives.

    Those miserable events have been painted vividly on the national memory: the red coats with their smart tri-cornered hats and lethal muskets facing down a squad of kilted, porridge-scoffing Highlanders, brandishing targes[1]
10   and broadswords that wouldn't have looked out of place in the Iron Age.

    Nor is it an entirely erroneous picture. The Highlanders who rallied to the Jacobite cause would certainly have looked much as today's Taliban fighters do to British soldiers in Afghanistan. With their heavy plaids, Old Testament beards and couthy, woollen headgear, they would have presented a distinctly
15   homespun picture. But appearances can be deceptive. Charles Edward Stuart's men might not have been elegant, but in military terms they were far from hand-knitted.

    So says Professor Murray Pittock of Glasgow University who has come upon evidence, while updating his book, *The Myth of the Jacobite Clans*,
20   showing that this army was as sophisticated in weaponry as the Duke of Cumberland's forces. Pittock believes the battle's outcome can be attributed not to an unfair struggle between swords and guns but to the Jacobites being outnumbered, the ground treacherous and the enemy's cannons better suited to the day than their own. As Pittock says: "Jacobites believed real soldiers
25   used muskets – 2320 Jacobite muskets and 190 swords were picked up from the battle-field. That's more than 10 to one."

    You can almost understand why the Jacobites were portrayed as tribal warriors. Their political aims were supported only by a minority and threatened chaos, if they won the day.

30   More than that, though, the epithet of savage may have been an attempt to reflect the barbarity of Culloden itself, one of the grimmest and most ignominious battles in Scotland's long history of grim and ignominious battles. Ragged, fierce, many not even speaking English, this army was easy to caricature. But that doesn't fully explain it. Generation after generation,
35   Highlanders have been portrayed as dim-witted and hot-tempered. The massacre of Glencoe, half a century before Culloden, horrified genteel lowland society but the MacDonald clan was nevertheless depicted as thrawn, cunning and fatally naive: in other words, authors of their own misfortune.

    From the earliest records, the Highlander was seen as backward and
40   scary, a creature apart from the rest of the race. And this cruel stereotype has become a neat shorthand for city dwellers uneasy about their northern compatriots, a feeling fuelled more by fear than by superiority.

At least, if there is a sense of superiority, it is utterly misplaced. In fact, I'd argue that Highlanders are probably having the last laugh. Not only do they

45   enjoy some of the finest scenery in Europe, but as technology advances they are as well-connected to the globe as those of us sweating away in polluted cities. That, however, is the least of it. The canniest folk have realised the Highlands are the best place to live because overnight the very things that once made the Highlands so intimidating, and their people so alien, have

50   become priceless.

In this ecologically stressed age – when pressure on fuel, water and space is growing so fiercely it feels as if the walls and ceiling are closing in upon us – the Highlands have an abundance of all these. Want to build an extension? There'll be no quibble about finding a few extra square metres. Need to get

55   a turbine whirling? Wind is unlimited. Always wanted a stove in the living room? There'll be peats aplenty to keep it alight. Worried a dry summer could ruin the lawn? Drought won't be a problem; mud-slides, snow-melt and flooding perhaps, but not hosepipe bans. But what about that blight on the summer season that sees tour buses burning rubber as they flee the

60   Cairngorm sunset? Well, almost as many funds are being devoted to the midge problem as to Heathrow's new runway. From traps and pesticides to starvation, the Highlands' only true savage is under attack. And even if it should remain resistant to science, the midge is migrating ever southwards. So one day we may be looking north from beneath our West Lothian

65   mosquito nets, wondering why we didn't catch the last train to Pitlochry.

I could, of course, start talking about the values of community spirit, of the enterprising can-do attitude of many Highland villagers, and the sense of belonging that small towns in the middle of nowhere can bring. About what a great place to bring up kids. But to do that would make me sound

70   soft, sentimental and southern, and if there's one thing that distinguishes the Highlander, it's hardiness.
You can call that savage if you like. I prefer the word smart.

[1]targes – an archaic word for shield.

PASSAGE 2

In this extract from his book, The Lion in the North, John Prebble describes the horrors of the Battle of Culloden and the real tragedy for the clans.

1　At dawn on Wednesday April 16, 1746, fewer than five thousand hungry and exhausted men limped into their battle-line on a bleak moor above Culloden House – clansmen, foothill tenantry, and a few newly-arrived Irish and Franco-Scots. A gale was now driving sleet into their faces, and they

5　stood upon ground which no senior officer but Charles believed could be defended. Below on the Moray Firth to their left were English transports and men-of-war, and advancing toward them from Nairn were nine thousand men under the Duke of Cumberland, sixteen battalions of foot and another of militia, three regiments of horse and a company of artillery. Three of the

10　regular battalions were Lowland Scots, a fourth and the militia had been largely raised from Clan Campbell. Within an hour of noon the battle was over. Winnowed by Cumberland's guns, the clans at last charged through musketry and grape, and where they could reach the enemy they slashed their way into three ranks of levelled bayonets. Held back by volley-firing,

15　Clan Donald did not engage the right of the red-coat line, and the men of Keppoch, Clanranald and Glengarry tore stones from the heathered earth and hurled them in impotent fury. The stubborn withdrawal from the charge became an hysterical rout, and the British marched forward to take ceremonial possession of a victorious field, bayonetting the wounded before

20　them, and cheering their fat young general. The long brawl of Scottish history had ended in the terrible blood of its best-remembered battle.

　　This time the policy of repression was inexorable. It began immediately with an order for the extermination of the wounded who still lay upon the field. It was continued by the harsh imposition of martial law, the shooting

25　and hanging of fugitives, the driving of stock, the burning of house and cottage. Lowland and English graziers came to Fort Augustus to buy the cattle driven in from the glens, and the Navy and the Army co-operated in a ruthless search for the fugitive prince, brutalizing those who were thought to have information about him, and hanging a few who would not give it.

30　In this sustained terrorization, Lowland regiments were as active as men from English shires, and three officers long remembered for their bitter cruelty were all Scots. The only government forces to show compassion for the homeless and the hunted were the Campbell militia from Argyll. The prisoners taken were tried in England, lest Scots juries be too faint-hearted.

35　The axe was nobly busy on Tower Hill, and the gallows rope sang at Carlisle, York, and Kennington Common. One hundred and twenty common men were executed, a third of them deserters from the British Army, but nearly seven hundred men, women and children died in gaol or in the abominable holds of Tilbury hulks, from wounds, fever, starvation or neglect, Two

40　hundred were banished, and almost a thousand were sold to the American plantations.

　　This time, too, the structure of the clan system was torn down and left to its inevitable decay. The Clansmen were stripped of the tangible manifestations of pride. When the proscription on Highland dress was lifted

45　in 1782, few of the common people accepted it. It became the affection of their anglicized lairds, the fancy dress of the Lowlanders, and the uniform of the King's Gaelic soldiers.

The wearing of a red coat, a belted plaid of black government tartan, enabled the young men of the hills to keep some of their pride, and to follow
50 the military example of their ancestors. Their eagerness and their valour were prodigally expended by successive governments. They were raised in the old way of clan levies, each chief and his tacksmen bringing in so many of their young tenants, by persuasion or by force. They were a unique and splendid corps. Crime and cowardice were rare, and when they mutinied, as they
55 sometimes did, it was with dignity and because the promises made to them by their chiefs had been broken by the government.

The last tragedy of the clans may not be the slaughter of Culloden, but the purchase and wasteful expenditure of their courage by the southern peoples who had at last conquered them.

Questions on Passage 1

Marks Code

1. Read lines 1–6.

  (a) What two reasons does the author give for claiming that 'Culloden Moor is the bleakest place on the planet'?   **2** **U**

  (b) Read the third sentence (lines 2–4). Show how the writer's use of sentence structure reinforces her opinion of Culloden Moor?   **2** **A**

2. Read lines 7–10.

Show the writer's use of language conveys her opinion of 'those miserable events' (line 6).   **4** **A**

3. In your own words, explain what the writer means by 'a distinctly homespun picture' (lines 14–15).   **2** **U**

4. Read lines 18–26.

According to Professor Murray Pittock, what were the reasons for the Jacobite failure? You should use your own words as far as possible.   **3** **U**

5. Read lines 35–38.

In what ways, according to the author, were the MacDonald clan 'authors of their own misfortune' (line 33)? Use your own words as far as possible.   **3** **U**

6. Read lines 39–42.

Show how the paragraph between lines 34 and 37 performs an important linking function in the writer's argument.   **2** **A**

7. Read lines 51–58. ('In this ecologically stressed age... hosepipe bans.')   **4** **A**

Show how the writer's use of language conveys a more attractive picture of the Highlands.

8. Read lines 66–71.   **5** **U**

Using your own words as far as possible, outline **five** important points that are made to develop the writer's argument about the advantages of Highland living.

9. To what extent does the final paragraph form an effective conclusion to the passage as a whole?   **2** **E**

(30)

Answer: She blames the Scots for having an inbuilt pretentiousness: that the Scots upper classes adopted unthinkingly the idea that the vernacular was a signal of belonging to a lower social classes.

Commentary: In this case, the colon is signalling an explanation for the preceding statement, which makes the assertion that the decline in the Welsh and Scots languages was brought about by ingrained snobbery – that there was adopted unthinkingly by the Scots upper classes the idea that the Scots vernacular was a signal of belonging to the lower social classes.

HINT There are two main uses for the colon: to introduce an explanation for a preceding statement or to introduce a list. Although this isn't a punctuation question, the colon assists us in the reading process.

4. (a) This is again a meanings of ideas question, the answer to which lies in the sentence following. The underlining indicates where exactly the answer lies – all you have to do is put it into your own words: 'But we are not beyond the continuing fear that the richness of our language will disappear because of a failure to knit it more comprehensively through everyday transactions.'

Answer: The point she is making is that there is a worry that by not incorporating our vernacular language (1 mark) in our various institutions it could fall out of use. (1 mark)

Commentary: Although the idea here sounds complex, when you look closely at which she is saying, it's quite straightforward: there is a worry that by not incorporating our vernacular language in our various institutions it could atrophy (waste away / fall out of use).

HINT The question is really testing our understanding of 'richness of our language', 'failure to knit it comprehensively through' and 'everyday transactions'.

(b) This is a question about how the writer's use of imagery helps to make her point (above) clear. But the question also asks about effectiveness.

Answer: The image of knitting literally means the joining of strands of wool closely together, which entirely supports her idea of intertwining or joining together the vernacular language with the language of institutions.

> **TOP EXAM TIP**
>
> In questions about the effectiveness of imagery, you *must* first of all explain the *literal meaning* of the image, then go on to explain how it helps convey meaning in the context.

Commentary: The effectiveness of an image is whether or not they do clarify / enhance the point being made. The image here is fairly obviously 'a failure <u>to knit it</u> more comprehensively through' Let's now deconstruct this image: the verb 'knit' means literally to intertwine wool using needles (or a machine) in order to create a woollen item of clothing. Here, the idea of interlocking applies – she is suggesting that the vernacular dialect be interwoven, intertwined with everyday transactions to create something new and useful – so it means to join strands closely together, which entirely supports her idea of intertwining or joining together the vernacular language with the language of institutions.

HINT The first thing you must do is identify the image – and be careful because metaphors can be implicit. For example, in the phrase – he was hedged in – you might not spot the metaphor, the comparison between where he was and being enclosed in the way in which hedges enclose fields and gardens.

5. (*a*) The phrase 'Structural significance' is not as unfathomable as it sounds. Just use your common sense. What is the purpose of the question? It allows her to answer it. But it also links what she said before to the answer she is about to give.

Answer: The structural significance of this question is that it links what she said at the end of the previous paragraph to this paragraph. (1 mark) By asking why we should bother about incorporating the Scots language into the fabric of professional institutions, she allows herself the opportunity of answering it, thus giving the reader all the reasons for bothering. (1 mark)

Commentary: The 'Why should we bother?' undoubtedly leads on from the idea in the previous paragraph about the fear of the disappearance of the Scots language by not incorporating it into our institutions. By asking why we should bother (about incorporating the Scots language into the fabric of professional institutions) she allows herself the opportunity of answering it, thus giving the reader all the reasons for bothering.

 HINT Questions about the structure of paragraphs or, as in this case, about the structure of a question at the beginning of a paragraph have often to do with linkage.

(*b*) All you have to do is list the ways in your own words. The ways can be found in the following bit of text: (1) Language reflects our cultural experiences and offers layers of particularly evocative meanings to our lives. (It is no accident that Scots has so many terms for rain and general climatic dreichness.) To understand and value this is not to enter into some kind of sterile argument about the linguistic hierarchy. This is not about Scots versus English, or Scots versus Gaelic; (2) it is a celebration of our rich diversity which brings us vivid, though not interchangeable, versions of Scots from rural Aberdeenshire to Galloway and its many variations in our cities. (3) But it doesn't just weave colour into the national tapestry; according to the conclusions of the recent audit, an increased status for Scots also brings important economic consequences.

Answer:
1 Dialect expresses and enhances various aspects of our everyday lives and society;
2 Dialect marks the huge variety of local use of language throughout all the geographical areas and cities of Scotland;
3 There are valuable financial benefits wherever and whenever the local Scots language is taken seriously.

Commentary: In this appropriate section of the paragraph she makes three main points, each of which is elaborated. When you summarise, you can omit the elaborations. But remember to use your own words!

HINT In these summarising-type questions, the number of marks is a good guide to the number of points you should make.

6. Let's look at the stretch of text. Appropriate aspects of sentence structure have been underlined for you: 'Self-evidently, having a greater presence in the classroom and the media is important, but both ourselves and the Welsh could do worse than examine the lessons of Ireland, where attempted compulsion via immersion <u>in schools, regional development policies, civil-service publications and standardisation of spelling and usage</u> <u>stubbornly failed to restore the primacy of Irish Gaelic</u>.'

Answer: There are two main ways in which the writer uses sentence structure to support her point that immersion via compulsion fails.

i) By placing 'Self-evidently' at the very beginning of the sentence, she draws attention to its meaning – that she is admitting that there should be a greater presence of the language in the classroom, but by making this concession to having language in schools and the media, she devalues its impact on her final conclusion; (1 mark)

ii) The list 'in schools, regional development policies, civil-service publications and standardisation of spelling and usage' helps express the extent and variety of places where compulsory immersion has been introduced and failed in Ireland; the list also helps delay the climax, making it all the more effective by drawing attention to her main point that the compulsory introduction of immersion fails. (1 mark)

Commentary: There are various points to be made about her use of sentence structure in this part of the paragraph:

(a) 'Self-evidently' is placed at the very beginning of the sentence, thereby drawing attention to its meaning – that she is admitting that there should be a greater presence of the language in the classroom, but by drawing attention to it, she devalues its impact on her final conclusion;

(b) The clause 'having a greater presence in the classroom and the media is important' not only explains what is self-evident, but it also effectively delays the climax of the sentence;

(c) The list 'in schools, regional development policies, civil-service publications and standardisation of spelling and usage' helps express the extent and variety of places where immersion has been introduced; the list also helps delay the climax, making it all the more effective;

(d) the expression 'stubbornly failed to restore the primacy of Irish Gaelic' which is the consequence of the 'attempted compulsion via immersion' policies, is the climax of the sentence.

(e) The entire sentence is inverted, the main point coming at the very end, thus creating greater impact.

All of these aspects of sentence structure support her point that the policy of immersion via compulsion failed. Since there are only 2 marks you only need make two of the above points.

> **HINT**
> Only 2 marks are available, therefore you need to identify two basic points about sentence structure or one elaborate point, showing that her point that compulsion via immersion does not work. 'Immersion', when used about language teaching, means that you instruct the pupil in the language to be learned.

7. The answer lies in the expression that people need to be enthused rather than compelled to rediscover the joys of hearing themselves in their own voice.

Answer: The lesson from Ireland is that it is more effective to encourage people to use their local language than it is to try an compel them. (1 mark)

Commentary: This is a fairly straightforward meaning of ideas question – it is more effective to encourage people to use their local language than it is to try an compel them.

8. The phrase 'To what extent' means that you are, of course, free to say that it is not an apt conclusion.

Answer: The final sentence is quite apt since it draws on people's fear concerning the continual complaints from all quarters about standards of spelling (1 mark), and the use of the Scots word 'scunner' is very appropriate for a passage on Scots language. (1 mark)

Commentary: The final sentence is quite apt since it draws on continual complaints from all quarters about standards of spelling, and the use of the Scots word 'scunner' is very appropriate. Moreover, the final word 'scunner' is an excellent reminder for the reader of what the passage has been about. Also by beginning the sentence with 'And', the writer draws attention to its being the final point – highly apt for a conclusion!

PASSAGE 2

9. (a) A fairly straightforward question, the answer to which lies clearly in the text: 'since I hold fast to the horribly unfashionable view that <u>learning by rote</u> is extremely good for children.'

Answer: Committing something to memory (1 mark) by constant repetition without necessarily understanding it. (1 mark)

Commentary: You have to be careful about this phrase because 'learning by rote' is not the same thing as learning something by heart. Learning, in this context, certainly means learning by heart, but 'by rote' means learning something repetitively, without necessarily understanding what you have learned.

> HINT Sometimes you have to work backwards from the phrase you've been given.

(b) You are given the tone – it is smugness. You have to analyse the language to say how her use of word choice creates it. Here is the relevant piece of text: 'Being able <u>to trot out</u> <u>yawning sections</u> of The Lady Of Shalott by memory <u>may not afford pleasure</u> to <u>someone forced to listen</u>, but it's oddly comforting that it will always be there. Similarly, most of my generation <u>take for granted</u> that we probably have at least a dozen long Burns poems permanently stored, ready to quote, mull over, or simply to recite to <u>blinking, uncomprehending non-Scots</u> should the occasion demand.'

Answer: 'may not afford pleasure' suggests that she recognises that others may not appreciate her recitations – but by implication it gives her pleasure and that's all that matters, a fairly conceited attitude; (1 mark). 'someone forced to listen' suggests that others may be so reluctant to hear her recitations that she has to force them to listen, but she isn't concerned about their feelings, an arrogant attitude revealing her lack of concern for others' feelings of boredom. (1 mark)

Commentary: Thee are several phrases that express this smug tone. Let's take them in turn:

(a) 'To trot out' suggests that she has no difficulty in reciting the poetry – it's all too easy for her;

(b) 'yawning sections' suggests that she feels others will be bored by her recitation, but she doesn't care – she still goes ahead;

(c) 'may not afford pleasure' suggests that she recognises that others may not appreciate her recitations – but by implication it gives her pleasure and that's all that matters;

(d) 'someone forced to listen' suggests that others may be so reluctant to hear her recitations that she has to force them to listen, but she isn't concerned about their feelings;

(e) 'take for granted' suggests in context that it's effortless for her and her generation to recite the poetry – they feel superior;

(f) 'blinking, uncomprehending non-Scots' suggests a superior, almost arrogant tone.

Any two of the above for 1 mark each.

10. (a) This is another meanings of ideas question, and in this case it is quite straightforward: 'But memorising text is only part of the process. Comprehension is considerably more important.'

Answer: It is more important to understand (1 mark) what has been learned by heart / committed to memory. (1 mark)

Commentary: The question is testing your understanding of the word 'comprehension', especially given the context. She has been talking about learning by rote, which you understand is learning by heart without necessarily understanding the memorised text. She now goes on to argue that it is more important to understand what has been learned.

(b) In this question you have to deal with both word choice and sentence structure: the task is to show how the writer uses both to reveal her delight in the poetry of Burns. 'How can anyone hope to enjoy the beauty, mischief and grace of Burns without having a working knowledge of the vocabulary, syntax and grammar that he employed to fashion his great works?'

Answer: Sentence structure

Moreover, the sentence is climactic in structure, the climax being delayed by two sets of lists: (1) 'the beauty, mischief and grace of Burns'; and (2) 'the vocabulary, syntax and grammar'. The climax 'his great works' reinforces her delight in his poetry. (2 marks)

> **TOP EXAM TIP**
>
> There are four kinds of sentences –
>
> 1 the statement: The boy sat the exam;
>
> 2 the interrogative (question): Did the boy sit the exam?
>
> 3 the imperative (command): Sit the exam, boy!
>
> 4 the interjection: Alas! (The boy failed the exam.)
>
> When you are asked about sentence structure, check first of all what kind of sentence you are being asked about. If it's a question, is the question rhetorical or is there an answer?

Answer: Word choice

'Beauty, mischief and grace' – the very words themselves suggest sheer delight ('beauty' suggests the magnificence of the writing, 'grace' suggests its elegance and stylishness, and the surprising 'mischief' suggests the often sardonic nature of his poetry), but the oxymoron (the juxtaposition of 'mischief' with the other two qualities) injects surprise into the list of adjectives, thereby highlighting her admiration for all the various qualities of the poetry of Burns. (2 marks)

Commentary: The question restricts the language features to word choice and sentence structure. Remember to identify the appropriate words or phrases and relate them to the task, which is to show how the writer uses these words to reveal her delight in Burns' poetry. With sentence structure, keep in mind all the possible structures (listed on page 5) and then show how the appropriate structure conveys her delight in the poetry.

Sentence structure

The sentence is in the form of a rhetorical question, which has the effect in this case of drawing attention to her argument that the delights of Burns' poetry are actually enhanced by knowledge of the Scots language, especially the vocabulary, syntax, and grammar that he used.

Moreover, the sentence is climactic in structure, the climax being delayed by two sets of lists: (1) 'the beauty, mischief and grace of Burns'; and (2) 'the vocabulary, syntax and grammar'.

The lists themselves are a structural device in their own right: both lists adopt the tripartite structure (tripartite structure is in the format: a, b and c), the rhythm of which is effective in drawing attention to meaning and it also adds to the climactic structure of the lists, praising the delights of Burns' poetry.

Word choice

'Beauty, mischief and grace' – the very words themselves suggest sheer delight ('beauty' suggests the magnificence of the writing, 'grace' suggests its elegance and stylishness, and the surprising 'mischief' suggests the often sardonic nature of his poetry), but the oxymoron (the juxtaposition of 'mischief' with the other two qualities) injects surprise into the list of adjectives, thereby highlighting her admiration for all the various qualities of the poetry of Burns.

That she is aware of the 'vocabulary, syntax and grammar' that he used to fashion 'his great works' reveals the she is so delighted with his poetry that she has taken the trouble to fathom how it works linguistically. The very term 'great works' shows her admiration and the esteem with which she regards his poetry.

> **TOP EXAM TIP**
>
> When analysing the climactic nature of a sentence, look for anything that delays the climax: lists, parentheses, the insertion of phrases, phrases at the beginning of the sentence.

4 marks available: two developed points, or one developed point and two basic points, or four basic points.

> **HINT** The sentence is in the form of a question. In this case the question is rhetorical – in other words, it does not require and answer simply because the answer is implied in the question.

is meant by 'a relentless omnipresent diet of pap' and by 'disguised as entertainment'.

> **HINT** With such questions, if you don't actually know the meanings of the word, don't leave a blank – try working the meaning out from the overall context.

(b) Careful – this is a question about the *underlying message* of children's tv, so we have to read the lines carefully.

Answer: The underlying message is both nasty and trivial (1 mark) – that all that matters is beauty and fame (1 mark).

Commentary: The writer makes the following point: 'the medium has been overrun with the vicious, shallow message that only good looks and fame count', which has to be put into your own words, for 2 marks.

> **HINT** You should know what is meant by 'subtext' and 'underlying messages'.

(c) This question isn't as easy as it looks – you really need to make reference to the text in order to demonstrate the contrast.

Answer: The writer's use of the contrasting expressions 'happily and innocently', 'desk-tidys' made from 'empty washing-up bottles' with 'no children's programme would dare recommend using empty toilet rolls', 'sue on hygiene grounds', 'everyone's got a dish washer' (for 1 mark) clarify her argument that television has transformed from its early days of innocence and simplicity to become a more worldly pseudo-sophisticated medium (1 mark).

Commentary: Here you are being asked to show how the use of contrast contributes to the writer's line of thought about television, therefore you have to identify the contrast then indicate the way(s) in which it contributes to her overall argument.

Let's look at the lines from the passage:

We look back to the days when we so happily and innocently spent afternoons making those aforementioned useful items: desk tidys, model farms, Christmas decorations.

Can you imagine? No children's programme would dare recommend using empty toilet rolls today because mothers would sue on hygiene grounds, and nobody has empty washing up bottles because everyone's got a dishwasher.

Now look for the contrasts: the expressions 'happily and innocently', 'desk-tidys' made from 'empty washing-up bottles', are being contrasted with 'no children's programme would dare recommend using empty toilet rolls', 'sue on hygiene grounds', and 'everyone's got a dish washer': these contrasts contribute to her idea that the early naive simplicity of television has been replaced by modern, worldly pseudo-sophisticated notions.

> **HINT** Questions about contrast can be quite tricky. Always read such questions very carefully so that you are clear about precisely what you are being asked to do.

11. Try to 'listen' to the tone – and you get the chance to justify your opinion.

Answer: The writer's tone is one of annoyance (1 mark). In the expression 'hardly a child born after 1990 who can be bothered cutting out cardboard and constructing *anything*' the use of Italics draws attention to her annoyance. Also the shortness and sharpness of the minor sentence 'Oh no' reinforces the point she is making and contributes further to her anger and exasperation (1 mark).

Commentary: Here you have to indicate what you think the tone to be, then justify your answer by reference to the text. You must make sure that you use textual reference to support whatever you claim to be the tone.

There are several possible answers! You can justifiably claim the tone to be dismissive, contemptuous, mocking, sarcastic. It could be regarded as one of annoyance, frustration, despair.

What ever you choose, make sure it is justified by reference to the text.

BOTH PASSAGES

12. Read the question carefully – here you are being asked to deal with ideas only.

Commentary: You can see then that it's possible that you are asked about **ideas** alone or **style** alone or both **style and ideas**.

You should also bear in mind that *style* covers all that *language* covers (word choice, sentence structure, punctuation, and imagery). But you should also consider *tone* and use of *examples* or *anecdote*.

The important factor in answering this question is to be highly specific: there are usually 5 marks for this question and it involves comparison – therefore you have to make at least two points about both passages – and each point must be supported by specific references.

If you are asked about *ideas* and *style*, you have to (a) demonstrate a clear understanding of both passages; (b) make sensible, specific, and perceptive comments on style; and (c) make some comments which clearly demonstrate the effect of the style – sensational, humorous, human interest, use of anecdote or illustrative examples. You can, of course, demonstrate the contrast in tone, if relevant, between the passages.

HINT Don't bother about which passage you actually preferred. It's better to choose the passage about which you can write most effectively – but don't forget this is about comparison. Write in sentences!

PRACTICE PAPER C   CRITICAL ESSAY WORKED ANSWERS

Section A – Drama

1. These are fairly common themes in plays, any one of which should apply to the play you have studied.

Commentary: Once you have chosen the theme, you have to demonstrate how it is established *and* developed – think about setting, characterisation, dialogue, symbolism, the usual techniques by which themes are established and developed. Although you will probably deal with only a couple of these techniques, nevertheless this part of your essay will no doubt take up much of your answer since there is a great deal to write about. But do not forget the second part – the means by which the theme is eventually resolved.

> **TOP EXAM TIP**
>
> Drama questions are deliberate set so that you can be fairly sure you will be able to use whatever text you have studied. If that text is 'Death of a Salesman', 'The Crucible', 'Hamlet', 'Othello', 'Streetcar', you should be able to find a suitable question.

HINT It is really important to read each question carefully – and this question points you to theme right away.

2. Note carefully what the question is asking you to do: you have first of all to explain the values of the society and then go on to say the ways in which the main character is out of tune with that society.

Commentary: Right away you can really need to choose a play where the conflict is between the main character and his or her society. That applies to a number of texts – 'Hamlet' who 'is out of joint' with the times in which he lives – he even says so. Proctor is out of tune with Salem society; Othello is very much out of tune with Venetian society; Willy Loman is out of tune with modern society – the scene with the wire recorder is one piece of evidence of that.

HINT In this case the majority of your essay is probably going to be where you demonstrate the various ways in which he/she is out of tune with the society – it's really a character question.

3. This is quite a common question, which occurs each year in slightly different formats.

Commentary: In Shakespeare, the central scenes usually occur in Act III, but in whatever play you have studied think carefully about which scene somehow changes the direction of the action and therefore of character.

> **TOP EXAM TIP**
>
> It's a good idea in your preparation for the exam to choose a scene or scenes that you feel are central or pivotal and work out in what way they contribute to theme and/or character development.

Be sure to choose a scene where there really is some kind of 'turning point' that affects characters and ultimately the development of the these.

4. This is also quite a common question, which means you need to know (a) where the ending begins; and (b) how the drama ends.

Commentary: In tragedies, the audience is invariably prepared for the ending – there is something that happens earlier in the play to alert us to the possibility of the death of the protagonist. Hamlet, for example, kills Polonius and comments that he will 'answer well the death (he) gave him'. Perhaps what is so moving / disturbing about the endings is the use of language: the poetry at the end of all four of Shakespeare's tragedies is highly emotional, as is the ending of 'The Crucible'.

 The question is asking about an ending which you found moving or disturbing. It is difficult to think of a play that doesn't fit this idea since the ending of tragedies is usually disturbing – all those deaths; and the ending of comedies is often moving – all those marriages!

Section B – Prose

Prose Fiction

TOP EXAM TIP

Check the novel you are studying: is the narration omniscient narrator, third person narrator, first person narrator – and how does that contribute to theme?

5. It's always a good idea to be prepared for this kind of question – and if you have studied your novel properly you'll know the method and how it contributes to the overall theme.

Commentary: The method of narration is extremely important in any novel or short story – where the novel is most likely to be in first person narration or omniscient narration, the short story is more than likely to be third person narration, but check!

First person narration usually means that we get to know and like the narrator but it has the in-built problem that the narrator has to be present in every scene or else he has to rely on other characters telling him/her what happened elsewhere or before the novel began 'The Great Gatsby' for example, uses flashback and flashback within flashbacks so that Nick Carraway can find out what happened previously.

Most of your answer, however, will depend on showing *how* the method contributes to theme.

 Don't think of the short story as an easy option – to produce a good answer if you choose the short story, you really do have to know it very well – the theme and all the appropriate techniques.

6. Once again, this is a question which directs you straight away to theme, inviting you to discuss the techniques by which the theme is established and portrayed and *how* the theme is satisfactorily resolved.

HINT> You could well think about novels from earlier than the 20th Century for this question.

7. The comparative question – you need to choose short stories that are relevant.

Commentary: How have the writers created the element of surprise in each case? In 'Father and Son' by Bernard MacLaverty, there is a slow revelation of the relationship between the unnamed father and his rebellious son – but the ending not only comes as a surprise, it brings a whole new dimension to the story and, in a real sense, opens up its theme. It could be beneficial to choose for this question two stories by the same author since there is likely to be a similarity in theme and approach to theme. On the other hand, you may well know a story that would contrast well in ending but share the same theme.

8. This is the particular / universal question. You need to talk about the story itself and its wider theme.

Commentary: 'The Great Gatsby' for example is, above all, a love story; it tells the story of Jay Gatsby's passion for Daisy Buchanan and his unrelenting quest for her love. She rejected him five years previously because he was too poor, and now, as the novel unfolds, we discover that he dedicated those years to acquiring sufficient wealth to satisfy her earlier criticism of him. Sadly his love for her remains unrequited.

But, perhaps more importantly, the novel also is an exploration of the corruption of the American Dream. The American Dream is enshrined in the American Constitution – that every American citizen is entitled to the pursuit of health, wealth, and happiness, though, of course, since there is only a finite amount of wealth to go around and since people have varying skills in achieving it, the consequence is that some will accumulate more wealth than others. Though much American literature deals with the problems of the American Dream, this novel is explores the idea that wealth does not in itself provide happiness, either for those who inherit wealth or those who achieve it, illegally or otherwise, by dint of their own efforts. Daisy, we discover, is the enshrinement of the American Dream – wildly rich but unobtainable. Thus the particular love story takes on a universal theme.

There are other related themes, such as the illusion of glamour, and the theme of dishonesty, both of which are related to the corruption of the American Dream. But perhaps the most important theme is the disintegration of moral values and the spread of social sterility.

Prose Non-fiction

9. You need to choose your non-fiction work carefully since not all non-fiction prose is gripping and exciting.

Commentary: In answering this question it is really important to discuss the ways in which the writer presents his or her ideas in a stimulating / exciting way.

 HINT In the instruction, note that the word 'stimulating' is used – but since you have been asked to choose a non-fiction text that you found 'gripping and exciting' you perhaps have to interpret 'stimulating' as inspiring rather than just thought-provoking.

10. This question offers wider scope since the instruction is to show how it captured your interest – in other words, discuss which techniques are used to engage the reader's interest in the subject.

Commentary: The writers of many biographies, autobiographies, travel books, and essays are particularly skilled in engaging reader's interest – but since here you are asked to deal with an issue, you are more likely to be successful in discussing an essay or piece of journalism.

 HINT Orwell is particularly skilled in engaging the reader's interest by means of a number of techniques including structure, climax and anecdote.

11. You need to be sure what is meant by 'an historical perspective': there are, however, many books that look back on a previous period in time – the days of Ancient Rome or even some periods in our history.

Commentary: Possibly there are very few such texts taught, but if you are tackling this question, then structure will be an important technique – looking at the ways in which the historical perspective has been created.

HINT You need to avoid a text which is just simply set in the past – it has to be a text that looks back on a previous era.

Section C - Poetry

12. There are many such poems that would fall into this category!

Commentary: Most probably, you would want to deal with both parts of this question together since the way the poet portrays the truths is most likely that way that he or she makes them shocking. The truths can hardly be separate from the ways in which they have been presented.

You should perhaps have a look at the poetry of Tony Harrison, who is particularly skilled at presenting shockingly unwelcome truths.

HINT A great many 20th Century poets deal with truths that are shocking or disturbing, but what matters here is the way in which the poet portrays the truths and makes them shocking.

13. In a sense, this is the obverse of the previous question.

Commentary: Believe it or not there are some happy poems! What you want to look for is a poem that celebrates some occasion, and some of Shakespeare's sonnets are written to celebrate beauty and love.

HINT The same advice as above – it is difficult to separate the portrayal of the experience from the ways in which the poet makes it happy.

14. This is a question about a narrative poem – a poem that tells a story and has a plot.

Commentary: Many ballads relate a story in a poetic form as do many poems from last century. Perhaps one of the most famous narrative poems is 'Tam o'Shanter' by Robert Burns, and one that you probably know quite well is 'Out, out –' by Robert Frost.

Rhyme plays a huge part in narrative poetry, therefore to answer this question well you really have to deal with rhythm and rhyme.

15. This question is really crying out for a poem written by one of the Romantic poets of the 19th Century.

Commentary: Many of the Romantics, particularly Keats, deal with the senses – the beginning of Ode to Autumn, for example, or Ode to a Nightingale all have powerful sensuous images.

SECTION D – FILM AND TV DRAMA

16. This should give you plenty of opportunity since so many novels have been made into films.

Commentary: Note carefully that you have to deal with both characters and setting – not plot. In a sense that makes it easier, since many film adaptations change plot considerably, while recreating character and setting very close to the original. You should think carefully about the ways in which setting has been achieved – and the extent to which devices have been use to recreate it as accurately as possible. One important leitmotif (a recurring symbol or theme) in the novels of Thomas Hardy, for example, is the tiny character in the huge empty landscape – that is a motif that film can reproduce very accurately.

17. Very often, particularly in TV dramas such as 'The Bill, there is a subplot which echoes, reflects and contributes to the main plot.

Commentary: Here you need to show how, in a series or film with which you are familiar, subplot is used to reflect or make a comment on the main plot. You are asked to show how that contributes to theme.

18. Stereotyping is an important tool to film and TV programme makers as it can be a shorthand way of presenting character or situation.

If you want to present a Scot on TV, how most effectively can you do it? Use a stereotype. That's what this question is about. To what extent do film and TV programme makers rely on stereotype, say at the beginning of the film or TV programme to communicate where it is going to be set or what mood is to be evoked? It's the same with character. You have to discuss the ways in which this kind of stereotyping enhances theme.

19. The dilemma can be about anything – but most likely it will be a moral dilemma.

Commentary: It's best if the dilemma is genuine – where the audience can see that there is a real difficulty involved. The most important (and rewarding) part of the question is showing the extent to which the audience's sympathy is engaged for him or her. What techniques have been used to make sure that, whatever choice is made, it will be the choice that the audience wants the character to make?